7 Days & Beyond
In
GRAND TETON
NATIONAL PARK

This mama moose with her calf was spotted on our Snake River raft trip in the spring. She appeared to be coaxing her calf to cross the river with her.

ON THE COVER: The trail above Jenny Lake leading to Hidden Falls, Inspiration Point, and Cascade Canyon.

7 Days & Beyond
In
GRAND TETON
NATIONAL PARK

Kendra Leah Fuller

HAP
HUDARI PUBLISHING

HUDARI PUBLISHING

ISBN 10: 0996149929
ISBN 13: 978-0-9961499-2-1

Printed in the United States of America

The author has made every attempt to provide accurate telephone numbers, addresses, and website addresses at the time of publication. Neither the publisher nor the author assume any responsibility for errors or for changes that occur after publication. The publisher and the author do not have any control over and do not assume responsibility for third-party websites or their content.

Dedicated to the grandeur that is Grand Teton National Park.

CONTENTS

ACKNOWLEDGMENTS

I would like to thank my family for their support and encouragement. To my parents, thank you for introducing me to Grand Teton National Park as a teenager. To my husband and children, thank you for taking our many research trips to the park and understanding why it is so hard to make me go anyplace else on vacation. I am glad you all love the park as much as I do. Unless otherwise noted, all images in this book appear courtesy of the author.

INTRODUCTION

I fell in love with Grand Teton National Park in the summer of 1981 while on a family vacation. I was 16 years old when I first laid eyes on the Grand Tetons' beauty and they have been calling me back ever since. As we leave Dubois and start the climb through the Shoshone National Forest towards Togwotee Pass, I am still on the edge of my seat with anticipation just like the 16 year old girl I once was. Every bend in the road holds the possibility that this just might be the one to reveal the spectacular beauty which awaits.

When that final curve opens the curtain to the Teton Range in all of its majesty, my eyes still fill with tears at the beauty before me. It is a wondrous site to behold. What must it have been like to be a fur trapper or explorer in the early 1800s who had just climbed one mountain range only to see the massive Tetons looming before them across the valley floor of Jackson Hole? I would have decided then and there that this is where my journey ends and taken out a claim at the base of the Tetons.

The many visits I have had in Grand Teton National Park have afforded me the opportunity to seek out places that the time constraints of only one vacation do not allow. There are sites and activities that I make time for on each visit, and those that are yet to be discovered. I have compiled a list of the top 10 sites, places, and activities that you will not want to miss if this is your first vacation here. For those of you who are returning visitors, I have included some of the "off the beaten path" places I have discovered.

In 2012, I was approached by a publishing company to write *Images of America: Grand Teton National Park*, a history of Grand Teton National Park told through the use of vintage photographs. I jumped at the chance to write the manuscript and learn more about the park's history. The struggle to designate the Teton Range, mountain lakes, and portions of the valley a national park became the focus of this book as I delved into my research. If not for the vision, perseverance, and philanthropy of a few, we might not have this beautiful park as we know it today. Hopefully, the history of the park and its struggle will come alive for you in *Images of America: Grand Teton National Park*.

This book is meant to be a stand-alone vacation guide and planner or a companion guide to *Images of America: Grand Teton National Park*. It is not by any means all inclusive of what Grand Teton National Park has to offer. There is still much to be discovered in the park and I look forward to returning time and again to make those discoveries.

Enjoy your vacation in the park! - *Kendra*

One

A PLACE FOR ALL SEASONS

Every season has something new and beautiful to behold in Grand Teton National Park. In planning when to visit, think about the activities you most enjoy and want to partake in. Some seasons are better suited to certain activities than others. Peak traffic in the park is during the summer months of June, July, and August. This also coincides with the most reliable weather. Yes, there will be a lot of other vacationers, although traffic is not nearly as heavy as it is in that famous park to the north known as Yellowstone National Park. If you want a little quieter trip, with fewer people around and less traffic, you may want to consider going just before or after the peak season. An advantage of this is also reduced rates at some lodging facilities. The disadvantage is that fewer places are open in the park outside of the peak season and the weather is not as predictable.

If this is your first trip to the park, I would highly recommend you plan your trip for late June to mid-August. If hiking in the higher altitudes is a priority for you, wait until August. Obviously, if you are planning your first skiing vacation to Jackson Hole disregard this advice! Jackson Lake is at its fullest in the spring after the snow melt. The level of the lake holds fairly well through June. Throughout summer, water from the lake is released through the dam to flow down the Snake River and provide irrigation for farm fields in Idaho. If there is a severe drought in Idaho, Jackson Lake water levels will be down by mid-August. In some years this is severe enough that lake activities departing from Colter Bay are closed along with the marina. First time visitors should plan to see Jackson Lake in front of the Tetons before the level goes down too far in August exposing the mud flats. It is still beautiful then, but some of the gorgeous lake reflections are no longer visible.

Other than the peak summer months, lodging is scarce inside the park although there are a few places open in the off season in and near the park. If you are planning on camping in the park, be sure and check ahead - not all campgrounds take reservations, some are first come first serve only. A few places in and near the park are open during the winter months for snowmobiling and other winter activities but most lodging is found in the town of Jackson this time of year. No matter what season you go, wildlife is abundant and the view is always spectacular

Spring

Springtime in Grand Teton National Park is glorious as the mountains and wildlife emerge from their winter hibernation. Mountain and valley streams and rivers are running full with the snow melt. Newborn leaves shimmer in brilliant contrast to their still exposed branches. When most of us think of spring, we think March, April, and May. Spring in Grand Teton National Park does not follow the norm. For the most part it emerges at some point in May and lasts into June.

Pronghorn antelope migrate back into the valley and bull elk can be spotted with new antlers in velvet. The elk herd is beginning its migration north after wintering on the National Elk Refuge near Jackson. Some will migrate as far north as Yellowstone National Park. Every spring since 1968, the Boy Scouts of America harvest the shed elk antlers from the Elk Refuge for the Boy Scout Antler Auction. Proceeds from the auction go towards maintaining and improving the Elk Refuge. Mama moose can be spotted with their calves. Black bears and grizzly bears bring their cubs down to the meadows and clearings. You should always be weary of bears in the park but this time of year some lower altitude trails may be closed due to increased bear activity. Please heed the warning signs and keep a safe distance from mama grizzly and her cubs.

Trumpeter swans, Canada geese, mallards, and common mergansers, are in various stages of nest building, incubating, and hatching their offspring. Oxbow Bend is a good place to catch sight of the trumpeter swans and their young along with other waterfowl and wildlife. Listen for the call of the sandhill crane which is amazingly loud across Jackson Lake. One of the sandhill cranes favorite nesting grounds is in the marshy areas near Jackson Lake. If you want to spot the sandhill crane, spend some time just north of the Jackson Lake Dam, scanning the marshes on both sides of the road. You may even get lucky and see this long-legged bird performing its courtship dance and claiming its nesting territory.

Water rushing under the footbridge on Taggart Creek from the spring snow melt along the Taggart Lake Trail, mid-May.

Cutthroat trout begin moving up the Snake River into the tributary creeks in preparation for spawning in early June. This time of year, the Snake River is running full and fast. The water is muddied with the debris it is carrying from the snow melt. If you are looking to fly fish on the Snake River, you will probably want to wait until early summer giving the river time to settle down and run clear again. After ice out in early spring can be a good time to try your luck fishing from shore on one of the parks beautiful lakes. Although you may not be able to enjoy trout fishing on the Snake River this time of year, the high water levels provide for spectacular whitewater rafting south of Jackson through the Grand Canyon of the Snake River.

Mountain flowers, like the arrowleaf balsamroot below, are beginning to bloom on the valley floor and lower elevation meadows. Keep your eyes open for other early bloomers like yellow violets, Nelson's larkspur, bluebells, Jacob's ladder, sagebrush buttercup, and biscuitroot while hiking. Hiking in the spring is limited to the lower elevations as this time of year deep snow is still present on the higher elevation trails. Only hikers trained and experienced in self-arrest techniques with a mountain axe should attempt to hike into the higher elevations at this time.

Arrowleaf balsamroot blooming in mid-May overlooking a pond on the Moose-Wilson Road. The ponds along this road are a good place to spot moose. The forest along each side of the road is also prime habitat for black bears. This is a narrow road open to bicyclists and passenger vehicles, no RVs.

Hikers should also be aware that avalanches can and do occur this time of the year. If you are looking to hike the higher elevations of the park, the trails will not be snow free until at least the second week of July, sometimes later. Postpone your trip until August if you are planning on hiking above 9,000 feet so you will not be disappointed. Weather can and does change quickly in the mountains. Make sure you are prepared for inclement weather. You do not want to be caught hours up a trail in shirtsleeves during a blinding snowstorm.

Summer

If you are planning your first trip to Grand Teton National Park, I highly recommend going in summer when all activities are in full swing and the weather is the most predictable. When speaking of summer in the park, I am referring to the months of July and August. June is still considered springtime in Teton country. Summer is the most popular time of year that people visit Grand Teton National Park and there is a reason. You could not ask for more beautiful weather. Daytime temperatures average around 80 degrees with cool, crisp mountain nights falling into the 40's. Brief, afternoon showers are typical with occasional thunderstorms but more than likely the weather will be overall fantastic, unlike spring and fall where you may spend a week in rain or snow. Be sure and pack the proper gear when hiking even if it is sunny when you set out in the morning. Weather conditions can and do change rapidly.

Blue Asteraceae blooming near Jenny Lake.

Meadow filled with yellow toadflax, blue asteraceae, and white engelmann asters near Jenny Lake in July.

One of the greatest advantages of visiting the park in the summer is that by July most mid to higher elevation trails will be snow free with the highest trails clearing by early August. Even with the crowds that come to the park this time of year, you will still be able to get away from everyone on the lesser traveled trails. Read, the higher you go, the fewer people you encounter! This is also the best time of the year for mountain climbing. The Snake River has calmed down after the snow melt and is now running clear and slower, providing for leisurely float trips through the valley. Wildflowers are in full bloom and abundant wildlife are roaming freely throughout the park.

If having a pool for the kids to play in is a priority, book your stay at the Jackson Lake Lodge as it is the only lodge with a pool in the park. Otherwise, you will need to book your room in the town of Jackson to accommodate your children or they can test the water temperature with their toe in one of the park's lakes. If you are planning a Jackson Lake boat ride, plan your visit for June or July. Colter Bay Marina may be closed at any time in August depending on how much water is being released from the lake for irrigation purposes.

Autumn glory at Oxbow Bend with Mount Moran towering in the background.

Autumn

Autumn in Grand Teton National Park is definitely my favorite time of year, despite the unpredictability of the weather. I have been snowed on as early as September 8 and had dry, gorgeous weather in early October with daytime highs in the sixties! The unpredictable weather is a bit of a trade-off but in return you are rewarded with the spectacular colors of fall foliage all around you. You will want to plan your trip for the 3rd or 4th week in September if you are going for the fall foliage. If you go too soon not enough color will have popped. Wait until October and many aspens and other trees may have dropped their leaves already.

Everything starts to wind down in the park in autumn, including the crowds of people. Although I have never felt like there were too many people in the summertime, I must admit I enjoy less traffic and fewer people rushing to view the wildlife. It really is a quiet time of year in the park. Many resorts are closed by the middle of September. The Signal Mountain Lodge stays open until the middle of October and offers reduced rates late in the season - not to mention it sits right on Jackson Lake. The Hatchet Resort sits just outside of the park and is also open into October. The reduced lodging choices also means your dining choices are limited, unless you want to drive into Jackson. Many guided activities also close down in mid to late September, such as the Jenny Lake boat ride to Hidden Falls, so check ahead before planning your trip to make sure you will be able to do the all of the activities you want to partake in.

Wildlife activity is abundant in the park and several species are mating. Listen for the bugle of the bull elk as he searches for his mates. Mama grizzly and her cubs can be spotted grazing in the meadows preparing for their long winter hibernation. As the water temperatures begin to drop, shore fishing on the park's lakes becomes active and the trout are biting in the Snake River before their spawn. Fishing is closed on Jackson Lake during the month of October and there are many other regulations to keep in mind when fishing in the park. If fishing is a planned activity, be sure to check out the rules and regulations ahead of time (www.nps.gov/grte/planyourvisit/upload/fishing11.pdf).

Winter

Jackson Hole is considered a premier winter sports destination. People from all over the world come here to enjoy downhill skiing, cross-country skiing, snowboarding, snowmobiling, snowshoeing, ice fishing, and more. Downhill skiing is centered near the town of Jackson at Snow King Mountain Resort and 12 miles northwest at Teton Village. Snow King, known as Town Hill by the locals, boasts the steepest north facing FIS racecourse in the Continental U.S. and is located just outside of Jackson in the Bridger-Teton National Forest. Skiing at Teton Village is on Rendezvous and Après Vous Mountains in the Teton Range with a vertical drop of 4,140 feet, one of the highest in North America. The more adventurous and advanced skiers can book guided backcountry skiing and snowboarding tours in Grand Teton National Park and the surrounding area.

Cross-country skiing and snowshoeing are very popular ways to enjoy the solitude of Grand Teton National Park in winter. The Moose-Wilson Road and Teton Park Road (from the Taggart Lake Trailhead to Signal Mountain Lodge) are closed to motorized traffic during the winter months. They are both open to cross country skiing and snowshoeing during this time and are intermittently groomed throughout winter. For a list of trails in and near Grand Teton National Park, download this PDF from the National Park Service (www.nps.gov/grte/planyourvisit/upload/XC-ski13.pdf) or take a ranger guided tour. Snowmobiling inside Grand Teton National Park is limited to Jackson Lake to provide access for ice fishing only and sled regulations apply. Guided snowmobile tours are available in the Bridger-Teton National Forest and Yellowstone National Park (www.nps.gov/grte/planyourvisit/upload/Snowmobile-brochure.pdf).

Anyone venturing into the backcountry should be aware that this is avalanche terrain. Pay special attention to avalanche forecasts and avoid known avalanche paths. You may be required to rent avalanche survival gear for guided backcountry adventures. When venturing out on your own into the backcountry it is recommended that you have an avalanche beacon, shovel, and probe pole.

Winter in Grand Teton National Park. Photo courtesy the National Park Service.

Two

TOP TEN HIGHLIGHTS FOR YOUR FIRST TRIP

There is so much to see and do in Grand Teton National Park that it is hard to recommend just 10 activities. I have visited the park many times over the years. There are some things I have only done once, many things I still have not done, and some things that I like to do every time I visit. The one that comes to mind as the biggest repeat offender is the Snake River scenic float trip. The mountains do not change but the river landscape does and there is always a new wildlife sighting. For these reasons, the float trip is definitely #1 on my list of "must do's" on your first trip to the park. I also highly recommend taking the boat ride across Jenny Lake to hike to Hidden Falls - this would definitely be my #2 recommended activity. Other than those top two activities, the remaining recommendations on my Top 10 List are in no particular order.

This is by no means an all-inclusive list of everything the park has to offer. You will find more activities and sites to see in the following chapter, "Beyond the Highlights." Depending on your personal interests, you might want to include these in your first trip or save them for your next visit. Many people fall in love with Grand Teton National Park and return year after year. Some of you will be arriving in Jackson Hole with a specific purpose in mind, such as skiing, mountain climbing, hiking, or fly fishing. You will find more information about some of these specific activities in later chapters.

View of the Grand Teton while floating down the Snake River.

Snake River Scenic Float Trip

While I am not going to rank all of the different activities in Grand Teton National Park, a scenic float trip on the Snake River is my number one must-do activity. This is a gentle ride down the Snake River with absolutely stunning scenery and photographic opportunities. There are no rapids and the trip is appropriate for all ages, from toddlers to the elderly. In the spring, when the river is running fast and full, the trip is a little bit quicker and the water is not clear. Experienced guides will prolong the trip by taking you down side channels that will be dry later in the season.

I have taken this trip down the Snake River five times now, the first being when I was 16 years old. I loved it so much and the guide was so cute that I managed to con him into a second (complimentary) trip down the river. I am tempted to include the picture my parents took of me with the guide, the huge grin on my face says it all.

This trip can be booked with most resorts in and around the park. You will meet at the resort and be transported to the launching point at Pacific Creek Landing or Deadman's Bar. You will float down the Snake to the historic Menor's Ferry District then be transported back to the resort. While you are enjoying the scenery, keep your eyes out for different wildlife on the shore and in the water. You may just spot a moose or grizzly stopping by to get a drink or cool off. Common mergansers and other waterfowl abound on the river. Look overhead to the tops of the pine trees, you have a very good chance of spotting a bald eagle nesting right above you. When the water is running clear you can see the trout below you in the river. I guarantee this is a trip the entire family will enjoy.

Lunch and dinner raft trips are also available through the Grand Teton Lodge Company resorts. Book online at gtlcreservations.com/vRes/Custom/Activities/ActivitiesAvailability. aspx or call 1-800-628-9988.

Interesting Tidbit: In 1886, four men arrived and set up gold prospecting operations on the Snake River near the Snake River Overlook and Deadman's Bar. Later that summer, three of the men were found weighted down with rocks near the bank of the river. One had been shot in the back and the two others had been killed with an ax. The surviving partner was tried and acquitted for their murders as there were no witnesses. Questions still surround this old west mystery which has become known as the Story of Deadman's Bar. Gold was never found but a half-mile long sluice was discovered at the site. Why would they go to this much trouble if there was no gold?

Hidden Falls, Inspiration Point, and Beyond via Jenny Lake

There are so many beautiful hiking trails in the park, it is hard to pick a favorite. However, one does rise above the rest as a must-do hike for the entire family, Hidden Falls. Turn west off of Teton Park Road at the South Jenny Lake Junction and park your car at the far end of the parking lot. You have two choices on how to begin your hike. Set out on foot from here and hike the trail around to the west side of Jenny Lake until you meet the Hidden Falls trail, approximately 2.5 miles. Or, walk down to the boat dock and hitch a ride to the bottom of the

The Grand Teton rising above the trail on the way to Hidden Falls and Inspiration Point.

Hidden Falls trail. From the boat dock you are only a half mile from the falls.

I recommend taking the shuttle boat across the lake. The boat is operational mid-May through late September and shuttles back and forth approximately every 10-15 minutes. Be sure and check the time of the last boat to catch a ride back across the lake. It is a beautiful ride across the lake and cuts off quite a bit of hiking time, keeping you fresh to hike past Hidden Falls another short half mile to Inspiration Point and beyond to Cascade Canyon from there.

The Hidden Falls trail is family friendly and definitely one of the most popular hikes in the park, for a reason. The falls are breathtaking any time of year, although they will be running at their most spectacular in the spring and early summer. The view over Jenny Lake and the valley of Jackson Hole from Inspiration Point is truly, well, inspiring. If you still have the legs and the time for it, continue on into Cascade Canyon. After a short distance of steeper climbing, the trail levels out to a much easier incline through the canyon. The people will also thin out as you hike beyond Inspiration Point. It is truly amazing to hike into this canyon with the Grand Teton and Mount Owen towering above you on one side and Mount St. John on the other. Be sure to listen for the sound of Cascade Creek rushing down the mountain to Hidden Falls.

If you want to venture into Cascade Canyon and possibly beyond to the highest elevation trails, be sure to plan your trip for late July or August. Cascade Canyon is at a higher elevation and in the spring and early summer, the trail may be packed with ice and deep snow. In fact, in the spring it is recommended that you carry a mountain axe, and be trained and experienced with self-arrest techniques. If there is snow on the trail watch your step as it can be deceptively deep underneath and unstable. You may find yourself in the snow up to your waist or higher! Yes, this did happen to my daughter and a gentleman we met on our raft ride.

If you are planning on taking the boat back across Jenny Lake, keep your eye on the time. You do not want to miss the last boat back and have to hike around the lake in the dark. As with any hike in the park be sure and make noise, have your bear spray immediately accessible, and know how to use it before you need it. Park rangers give classes on bear safety and how to properly use your bear spray. Be sure to drive the Jenny Lake Scenic Loop while you are here for spectacular views of the Grand Tetons across Jenny Lake.

Interesting Fact: Jenny Lake is named after the first wife of Beaver Dick Leigh, a local trapper and exploration guide to the Hayden Expedition of 1872. Leigh Lake, to the north, is named after Beaver Dick Leigh. These early expeditions into the area were responsible for many of the mountain and lake names. Many times they were named after a member of the expedition. The Grand Teton was actually rechristened Mount Hayden, after leader Ferdinand Vandiveer Hayden, but the name never took hold.

In the shadow of Mount Moran, up close and personal on the Jackson Lake breakfast cruise.

Jackson Lake Breakfast or Dinner Cruise

A cruise across Jackson Lake to Elk Island for breakfast or dinner is another reason to plan your summer trip no later than the beginning of August to ensure that the lake is still high enough for the Colter Bay Marina to be open. This is the only way, other than a really long hike, that you will get this close to the Teton Range on the west side of Jackson Lake. If the lake is calm, you will be treated to some of the most beautiful mountain lake reflections in the park. Whether the lake is calm or not, stunning photography opportunities await you.

Lake cruises are given by the Grand Teton Lodge Company and can be booked at your lodge or in advance online (gtlcreservations.com/vRes/Custom/Activities/ActivitiesAvailability.aspx). Your cruise will depart from the Colter Bay Marina. Listen to your captain for fun facts and folklore as you head out across Jackson Lake to Elk Island. You will enjoy delicious cowboy cuisine by the campfire. After dining, you are free to wander around on the island before heading back to Colter Bay. You will feel like you can reach out and touch Mount Moran! I recommend taking the chuck wagon breakfast ride through the Willow Flats and cruising across the lake for dinner.

View of Mount Moran and the Tetons from the chuck wagon breakfast site.

Horse Drawn Wagon Breakfast Ride

What could be better than meandering through the Willow Flats in a wagon on a cool mountain morning with spectacular scenery and wildlife to accompany you? My family has taken this ride and the Jackson Lake dinner cruise. They are both different yet spectacular. If you have time, do both. If not, save one for your next trip to the park. Book your wagon ride through one of the Grand Teton Lodge Company resorts.

Wagon rides depart from the Colter Bay Village corrals and travel leisurely through the Willow Flats to your breakfast site. Willow Flats is prime wildlife habitat. Bring your camera and be on the lookout for moose, bears, elk, deer, beaver and more. Enjoy some "cowboy coffee" with your delicious breakfast of ham, scrambled eggs, potatoes and flapjacks while you gaze upon the mountains. At certain times of the year, this ride may be closed due to grizzly bear activity in the Willow Flats. Rather than risks guests and bears, precedence is given to the bears. What bear could resist the smell of this delicious breakfast sizzling away? I do not think any of us want to grapple with a grizzly bear over breakfast!

Glorious summer reflection of Mount Moran in Oxbow Bend.

Oxbow Bend

The splendid reflection of Mount Moran in Oxbow Bend is every photographer's dream. The bend is located just over a mile east of the Jackson Lake Junction on Highway 89. There are two pullout areas from the highway where you can park your car, get out and relax for a while. Oxbow Bend is a very good spot for wildlife watching. In addition to abundant waterfowl like trumpeter swans, you may get lucky and spot a moose or grizzly bear coming down to the water's edge to get a drink or see some river otters frolicking in the water. Oxbow Bend is actually the old channel loop of the Snake River. Over time, the Snake cut its way through the neck of land formed by the loop and created a new river channel, leaving behind the tranquil waters of the bend.

Not far back up the highway to the west, you will see a stop sign on the south side of the road. Although it is not marked, this gravel road is referred to as Cattlemen's Bridge Road. There used to be a bridge at the end of the road from days gone by that ranchers used to drive their cattle across the Snake River. The road winds through an aspen grove and open meadow to a part of Oxbow Bend that you cannot see

Oxbow Bend near Cattlemen's Bridge.

from the main overlooks. It is very beautiful and secluded, well worth the side trip.

View of Mount Moran and Jackson Lake from Signal Mountain.
This photo was taken in 2013, a drought year with many forest fires.
You can see the haze of smoke settled in front of the mountains.

Signal Mountain Summit
At an altitude of 7,727 feet, the Signal Mountain summit is an ideal spot for panoramic vistas of the Grand Tetons on one side and the Snake River valley on the other. Visitors can choose to drive or hike to the top of Signal Mountain. Signal Mountain Road is located just south of Signal Mountain Lodge on Teton Park Road. The narrow, paved road climbs its way through the pine forest. Be on the lookout for wildlife and gorgeous views of Jackson Lake as you make your climb.

There are pullouts at the best photographic vantage points for your convenience. There are two parking lots at the summit. Be sure to stop at both. They offer different panoramic views of the Teton Range, Jackson Lake, the Snake River winding its way through the valley below, and the potholes left behind from the last glaciation period. If you are visiting the park in the early spring, take note that snow can be slow to leave Signal Mountain. The road to the summit may be closed until later in May depending on the weather. If the road is closed at the beginning of your trip, give it a few days and check back again to see if the road is open.

If you would like to hike to the top of Signal Mountain, park your car at the Signal Mountain Lodge parking lot and catch the trailhead from there. The hike to the summit is 3.7 miles one way and has some moderately steep inclines along the way. If you are hiking in spring, be sure to inquire about the condition of the trail before you start your hike. The trail can be snow covered and muddy into early summer. If you choose to hike the trail, you will be rewarded with some bonuses you will not have access to if you drive to the top. The trail passes along the shore of a small lake, before plunging back into the forest. You will pass through meadows and along streams. The trail gets rockier the further up you go and ends with a series of switchbacks before reaching the summit. Retrace your steps back down to Signal Mountain Lodge and satisfy the appetite you have worked up at the Trapper Grill.

Interesting Fact: Signal Mountain got its name when remittance man Robert Ray Hamilton, a great-grandson of Alexander Hamilton, went hunting in 1890 and never returned. Search parties were sent out with instructions to light a fire on the summit signaling they had found him. An unrecognizable body was found drowned in the Snake River and identified as Hamilton by his belongings. Mystery still surrounds his death. Some feel that he faked his own death while others think he was murdered by business partner John D. Sargent.

Keep your ears open when driving through the park. We heard this bull elk bugling on Signal Mountain and were able to spot him. We would have drove right past him if we had not heard him. Photo courtesy Paul Fuller.

Beautiful Teton reflections and the solitude of Taggart Lake await!
Photo courtesy Arielle Slobotski.

Hike to a Mountain Lake

There are many hiking trails leading to mountain lakes in Grand Teton National Park. You do not have to hike way up into the mountains to enjoy the beautiful rewards of these lakes. For ease of the trail and scenic reward, I highly recommend the Taggart Lake Loop.

The Taggart Lake Trailhead is located approximately 4-5 miles south of South Jenny Lake Junction on Teton Park Road. Taggart Creek flows from the lake along your trail, adding to the anticipation of reaching the lake. You will be rewarded with stunning views of the Grand Tetons reflecting in the lake. Pack a lunch and sit awhile in the solitude. From the Taggart Lake Trail you can choose to continue on another 1.5 miles to Bradley Lake or take the loop back down the mountain.

If you are looking for a longer day of hiking to see higher elevation lakes, continue on past Bradley Lake another 4-5 miles to Surprise and Amphitheater Lake. You can also reach these lakes from the Lupine Meadows Trailhead located north of the Taggart Lake Trailhead on Teton Park Road. One of the most popular higher elevation lakes is Lake Solitude. You can start this hike from the South Jenny Lake parking lot on the Jenny Lake Trail to the Hidden Falls

Trail, on to Inspiration Point, and up through Cascade Canyon. Head north at the fork at the top of Cascade Canyon to Lake Solitude at 9,032 feet elevation. You can cut 4 miles from this trip by taking the boat ride across Jenny Lake to the Hidden Fall Trail.

Another beautiful lake hike that is relatively flat is the String Lake hike at the inlet to Jenny Lake. You can hike past String Lake to Leigh Lake or cross over the footbridge and take the hike around Jenny Lake. The String and Jenny Lake hikes are very popular hiking trails. If you continue on past String Lake to Leigh Lake, you will notice a definite drop in hiker traffic. Emma Matilda and Two Ocean Lake are easily accessible from Pacific Creek Road which meets Two Ocean Road. From there you can park your car and hike around the lakes. If you are in the mood for

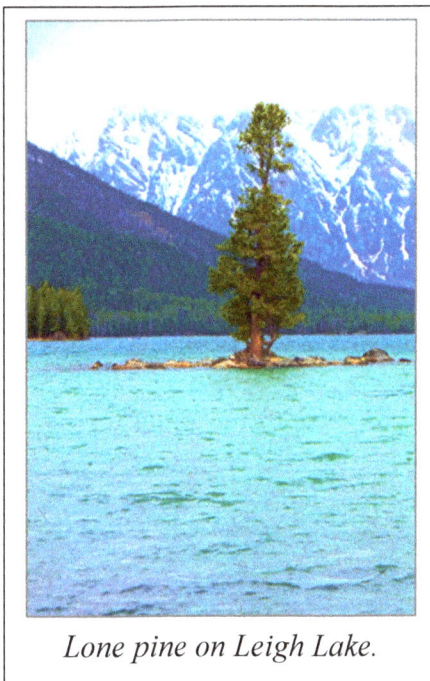

Lone pine on Leigh Lake.

a longer hike, park at the Jackson Lake Lodge and take the loop leading to Grand View Point then on past Two Ocean Lake and Emma Matilda Lake on the last leg of the loop.

There are many more mountain lakes accessible by hiking trails. Know your fitness and endurance levels. Always layer your clothing as temperatures and weather conditions can change rapidly. Take plenty of water with you and bear spray. Check to make sure the trails are open before you set out. Even lower elevation lakes and trails can be closed due to grizzly bear activity. When taking longer hikes, be sure to leave early enough in the morning to return before dark. Keep your eye on the time. If you realize you are not going to have time to make your destination and return safely home, turn around immediately. You do not want to risk your own life out in the elements or the lives of rescue personnel.

Fly fishing on the Snake River near Pacific Creek Landing.

Go Fishing

If you are a fisherman, you will not want to miss tossing your fly into the Snake River or trying to land a monster lake trout from a mountain lake. Guided fly fishing and Jackson Lake fishing excursions are available through several park lodges and local outfitters. Whether you are an experienced fisherman or a novice, taking a guided fishing trip will up your chances of catching fish.

If you are planning a Jackson Lake guided fishing trip, be sure to plan your trip no later than early August. Depending on the amount of water they are letting out of the lake for irrigation, the lake levels may be way down in August closing the Colter Bay Marina. You can also book a Jackson Lake guided fishing trip out of Signal Mountain Lodge whose marina is not as affected by the lake levels (307-543-2831). Please note that Jackson Lake is closed to fishing the entire month of October while the trout are spawning so plan your trip accordingly. Before fishing you will need a Wyoming fishing license.

Our family loves to fish. We have had really good luck fishing in the month of September. We have caught cutthroat and brown trout on the Snake River. We have also had good luck fishing from shore on Jackson and Jenny Lakes, where we caught lake, brown, and brook trout. Be sure to read the fishing regulation guide that comes with your Wyoming license. Only certain types of fishing and bait are allowed at different places within the park.

View of Jackson Hole from the top of the tram ride at Teton Village. Note the Snake River flowing through the valley and the Rocky Mountains in the distance.

Drive Scenic Moose-Wilson Road to Take the Tram

Half the fun of this excursion is the 8-mile drive down the Moose-Wilson road through the forest. If you are staying in the park, head south on Teton Park Road and exit the park through the South Entrance. Shortly after exiting the park, you will see the Moose-Wilson Road on your right. The road curves around and goes up a hill. At the top of the hill is a pullout which overlooks the ponds below. This is an excellent area to spot a moose and observe other wildlife. As you continue your drive, be on the lookout for all sorts of wildlife. We have seen moose in the marshy areas and beaver ponds, elk, and black bear cubs climbing in the trees. This is a narrow, winding road that is closed to all but automobile traffic - no RVs. It is also frequented by cyclists so please drive slowly. The road is closed during the winter and is typically open from May through October, weather permitting. It can also be closed due to grizzly bear activity so check the status before you plan your drive.

The Moose-Wilson Road exits the forest to the sagebrush flats and continues south along the Tetons. Turn west onto Teton Village Road, then north onto Village Drive and park in the parking lot. The tram leaves from the Jackson Hole Mountain Resort. Summer hours are from late May through early October, weather permitting. Be sure and call before you go to make sure the tram is open (307-739-2654).

You can't beat the view from way up here! At an altitude of 10,450 feet, on a clear day you can see for miles – past the Gros Ventres Mountains to the Rocky Mountains in the distance. Once at the summit, you can dine at Corbet's Cabin restaurant, hike the trails, mountain bike, and even paraglide. There are also scenic gondola and chair lift rides available in the summer from Grand Targhee and Snow King Mountain. Be sure to take a jacket along as it is quite a bit cooler on the summit than it is on the valley floor. When you are done, take in some souvenir shopping or a restaurant at Teton Village.

The Moose-Wilson corridor is home to many species of wildlife like this magnificent bull moose. In recent years, grizzly bears have joined the black bears in this area. In the fall of 2014, the road was closed to protect grizzly bears feasting on berries in preparation for their winter hibernation. Photo courtesy Paul Fuller.

View of the Grand Canyon of the Yellowstone River and Lower Falls from Artist Point.

Day Trip to Yellowstone National Park

If you have never been to Yellowstone National Park, it is only about a 40 minute drive away from Grand Teton National Park and I highly recommend taking a day to hit some of the highlights there. This is definitely a day trip as you do not get anywhere fast in Yellowstone (why would you want to?) due to the traffic and the massive size of the park. As in Grand Teton National Park, spring and fall are definitely less crowded. Head north on John D. Rockefeller, Jr. Memorial Parkway which takes you to the south entrance of Yellowstone.

The entire drive is beautiful. You will be amazed at how far north Jackson Lake extends, it seems to go on for miles and indeed it does. There are many pull-outs along the way providing ample opportunities for beautiful photographs of the Tetons and Jackson Lake from this vantage point. After passing Jackson Lake, you will start to descend towards the Snake River Valley. The Snake River flows into the north end of Jackson Lake and you will want to stop and take pictures of the valley before you cross the river and continue on to Yellowstone. The last gas station you will see for quite a while is located at Flagg Ranch shortly after you cross the Snake River. If you have not already filled the gas tank, you should do so now.

Before you know it, you will be climbing again. When we were in the park in 2003, this area had been recently burned in a large forest fire. We were absolutely amazed on our next visit in 2012 at the dense, new population of pine trees. A reminder that the forest renews itself. As you travel further north, the east side of the road will drop off. Look over the edge. You are looking down on a canyon carved by the Lewis River on its way to empty into the Snake River. You will definitely want to pull over at the overlook to take in the beauty. A little further up the road is Lewis Falls and Lewis Lake. Are you starting to understand the other reason you will not get through Yellowstone quickly? There is just so much beauty to see and revel in that you will want to set your mind for a relaxing day of driving with frequent stops to stretch your legs.

The park covers 3,472 square miles. At this size, you cannot do the park justice in one day. If this is your first trip to Yellowstone and you are only planning one day for the park, two must see attractions are Old Faithful and the Grand Canyon of the Yellowstone River at Yellowstone Falls. Shortly after you pass Lewis Lake, you will have the opportunity to swing into Grant Village for gas, snacks, and a restroom break. Before long, massive Yellowstone Lake will come into view. The lake encompasses 136 square miles and is the largest lake in the park. 22 miles into the park, the road forks. Stay to the left on the West Thumb and continue on to Old Faithful. When you arrive at Old Faithful go directly to the visitor center to check the clock for the next estimated eruption time. If you are lucky, you may have arrived within 10 minutes of this time. You do not want to miss this as the next eruption will be approximately 60-110 minutes from then. If you have just missed the most recent eruption, take time to grab a bite to eat, visit the gift shop, and explore the exhibits in the visitor center.

After viewing Old Faithful, continue north through Upper, Midway, and Lower Geyser Basins. There are walking trails throughout these basins. Take your time and enjoy Sapphire Pool at the Upper Basin, Grand Prismatic Spring at Midway Basin, and the Paint Pots of the Lower Basin. Be sure to heed the warnings and stay on the wooden trails throughout this area. You do not want to disturb this fragile ecosystem, and the ground can be unstable and dangerous to walk on.

From this area, continue north to Gibbon Falls for a picture taking rest stop. Before you get to Gibbon Falls, you will see the road to the West Entrance. Do not take this road, stay to the right and follow the road towards Norris. As with anywhere in these parks, be on the lookout for wildlife as you enjoy your scenic drive. At the very least, you are sure to spot the bison herd on your travels and quite possibly elk, moose, grizzly bears, and more.

When you arrive at Norris, take the road heading east towards Canyon Village. You are now on your way to the Grand Canyon of Yellowstone and the falls of the Yellowstone River. Turn south from Canyon Village and follow the signs to the falls. There are several pullouts that overlook the canyon and falls. Look for Inspiration Point, Grand View, Lookout Point, and Uncle Tom's Trail. One of the best vantage points is from Artist Point (photo above) and if I were only going to stop at one, this would be it. The canyon and falls are amazing. Be sure to stop at both the Lower and Upper Falls. The spectacular Lower Falls are 308 feet high plunging into the canyon which is up to 1,000 feet deep. While the Upper Falls may seem small in comparison, at 109 feet high they are still a very worthy site.

From the falls, continue south following the Yellowstone River through the Hayden Valley. You are on the last leg of your trip heading back to Yellowstone Lake. Enjoy the scenery and take a few moments to stop at Sulphur Caldron and Mud Volcano. When you get near Yellowstone Lake take time to stretch your legs and walk out on Fishing Bridge. While the original bridge was built in 1902, the existing bridge was constructed in 1937. Fishing is no longer allowed from the bridge but people used to line up along the bridge to catch cutthroat trout spawning in the river below. The bridge was closed to fishing in 1973 due to the decline in the cutthroat trout population but you can still look into the crystal clear water and watch the trout swimming below.

Your drive continues along the shore of Yellowstone Lake for another 21 miles until you meet back up with the road to the South Entrance of Yellowstone. Enjoy your drive back to Grand Teton National Park. You should make it back to the park in time to relax over a delicious dinner at your lodge.

Grand Loop of Yellowstone National Park

If you are up for a longer day of driving and want to take in most of Yellowstone's highlights, head north from Norris to Mammoth Hot Springs after visiting Old Faithful, the Geyser Basins, and Gibbon Falls. The terraces at the Mammoth Hot Springs are a unique and changing site formed by geothermal activity forcing hot water through the limestone and depositing minerals that form the terraces.

Also located in this area are the Albright Visitor Center & Museum and historic Fort Yellowstone built by the U.S. Calvary. Horace M. Albright was the superintendent of Yellowstone National Park and he dedicated many years of his life to the formation of Grand Teton National Park. Construction began on Fort Yellowstone in 1891. At this time, the United States Army had been protecting the park since 1886 and it became apparent that permanent facilities would be needed. They protected the park until the National Park Service was established in 1919.

From the Mammoth Hot Springs area, continue east to the Tower-Roosevelt area. Here you will find Petrified Tree and Specimen Ridge (on the northeast entrance road), the largest concentration of petrified trees in the world. If you have time, continue on this road into the Lamar River Valley. The valley provides excellent opportunities for wildlife viewing, including bison, elk, grizzly bears, coyotes, and wolves. If you do drive into the valley, you will need to turn and go back to the Tower-Roosevelt area, then continue south to the spectacular 132 foot Tower Fall of Tower Creek. Enjoy the scenic drive south after Tower Fall until you arrive at the Grand Canyon of the Yellowstone and follow the route above for the remainder of your trip.

Minerva Terrace at Mammoth Hot Springs along the Grand Loop. Photo courtesy NPS.

Use this as a bookmark or put it in your purse or pocket for a quick reference of daily activities. For your convenience, I have included another one in the back of the book.

Plan Your Trip To
Grand Teton National Park

- [ ] Snake River Raft Ride
- [ ] Jackson Lake Boat Cruise
- [ ] Chuck Wagon Breakfast Ride
- [ ] Relax for a while at Oxbow Bend
- [ ] Drive to the top of Signal Mountain
- [ ] Hike to Hidden Falls, Inspiration Point, Cascade Canyon
- [ ] Hike to a Mountain Lake
- [ ] Fly Fishing/Jackson Lake Guided Fishing Trip
- [ ] Moose-Wilson Road to take the Tram from Teton Village
- [ ] Take a Day Trip to Yellowstone National Park

www.WriterKendraLeah.com

Three

BEYOND THE HIGHLIGHTS

Now that you have scheduled the highlighted activities and sites into your vacation, you may want to fill in the gaps. There is so much to see and do in Grand Teton National Park that you will not possibly be able to do it all. Other activities to partake in depending on your interests are horseback riding, kayaking and canoeing, mountain climbing, golf, visiting different places for photo opportunities like Schwabachers Landing and the T.A. Moulton Barn on Mormon Row, exploring the myriad of hiking trails throughout the park, and just relaxing in the view.

If you are a history buff or curious about the way of life during the time of the first settlers, you may want to visit some of the still remaining cabins and homesteads in the park. Head to the Menor's Ferry Historic District to start your history trip off. Here you can visit Menor's Ferry, the Chapel of the Transfiguration, Maud Noble's cabin, and the Craig Thomas Discovery and Visitor Center. From there, head east to Highway 89 and turn north. Turn east onto Antelope Flats Road to visit Mormon Row, featuring the Moulton Barns and the Andy Chambers homestead.

After you have taken way too many pictures of the barns with the Tetons as their backdrop, continue up Antelope Flats/Gros Ventre Road into the Gros Ventre Mountains to view the slide that took place on Sheep Mountain. The slide formed Lower Slide Lake and almost two years later unleashed a tragic flood that nearly wiped out the town of Kelly below. Other notable cabins to visit are Cunningham's Cabin near Spread Creek where a deadly shootout took place, the Jim Manges Cabin located southeast of Taggart Lake and west of Cottonwood Creek, and the Lucas-Fabian Homestead south of Jenny Lake off of Teton Park Road.

Take a day to head south to the town of Jackson. On your way, visit the Lawrence S. Rockefeller Preserve, Murie Center, National Elk Refuge, and tour the Robert Miller homestead. Jackson is a western town with artistic flair. Downtown Jackson is full of art galleries, shops, and restaurants. While you are downtown, make a stop at the Jackson Hole Historical Society and Museum. The kids might enjoy a stop at Ripley's Believe It or Not and a trip down the alpine slide at Snow King Mountain Resort on the edge of town.

Take another day to head up to the northern end of the park. Visit the Colter Bay Visitor Center & Indian Arts Museum. Be on the lookout for grizzly bears and other wildlife in the meadows. The area near Pacific Creek Road is a favorite spot for grizzly bears. Stop and have a pizza at Leek's Marina and Pizzeria. Along this entire drive, you will be treated with amazing views of the Tetons behind Jackson Lake. You will be amazed at how many miles north Jackson Lake extends. One of my favorite hidden highlights is the drive up Grassy Lake Road to Polecat Creek which starts at the Flagg Ranch parking lot. No matter how you choose to spend your time in Grand Teton National Park, be sure to set aside time to just explore on your own and soak up the beauty.

The General Store at Menor's Ferry Historic District. Courtesy the National Park Service, photo by S. Zenner.

Menor's Ferry Historic District

Early settlers in Jackson Hole had to ford the Snake River which could be extremely dangerous. Seeing the need for a safer way to cross the river, William D. Menor settled on the west side of the Snake in 1892 and soon after constructed his famous ferry. The ferry was in operation until 1927 when it was replaced by a steel truss bridge. Menor enjoyed life as the sole homesteader on the west side of the Snake River until James Manges took up a homestead there in 1911. Manges' cabin is still in existence and can be viewed from the Cottonwood Creek picnic area or from the Taggart Lake Loop Trail.

The Chapel of the Transfiguration, below, is located in the historic district. The chapel was built in 1925 to serve guests at the valley's dude ranches. The picture window behind the altar was built to frame the Cathedral Group of the Tetons. Eight of the ten tallest peaks in the Tetons are included in the Cathedral Group with the three most popularly referred to in this group being the Grand Teton, Middle Teton, and Mount Owen.

Maud Noble's cabin is also in this area. Her cabin is the site of a historic meeting between locals and the superintendent of Yellowstone National Park, Horace Albright. Albright had a vision to make Grand Teton National Park a reality. This meeting resulted in the Jackson Hole Plan which proposed finding private individuals to purchase land and then donate it for a national park. They found their benefactor in John D. Rockefeller Jr. who purchased more than 33,000 acres of land in Jackson Hole that he later donated to the federal government with the express purpose of designating the land as a national park.

While you are in this area of the park, take time to stop in at the Craig Thomas Discovery and Visitor Center. In addition to a nice gift shop, the center has educational displays of the Tetons, ranger led hikes and tours of Menor's Ferry. If you need a bite to eat, be sure to stop at Dornan's complex of restaurants, shops, lodging, and gas.

The Chapel of the Transfiguration at Menor's Ferry Historic District. Photo courtesy the National Park Service.

The T.A. Moulton Barn is the most photographed barn in America and has become a symbol of Jackson Hole.

The Moulton Barns and Mormon Row

Thomas Alma Moulton and his brother John settled on Antelope Flats along Mormon Row in September of 1908. The T.A. Moulton barn above was a square structure when it was first built in 1913. Over time it evolved into the barn we see today. The barn is all that is left of the T.A. Moulton homestead. His brother John took up a neighboring homestead just to the north. John Moulton raised dairy cattle and sold milk and cream to nearby ranchers.

Many early settlers to Jackson Hole came from Idaho and Utah. Most of the settlers on Antelope Flats were of the Mormon faith. The settlers built their homesteads on either side of the road to make the best use of the land. This was a line village and it became known as Mormon Row. The Andy Chambers homestead is the only remaining nearly complete homestead in the park and it is located on Mormon Row. He took out his homestead in 1912 and completed the cabin in 1916. To visit this historic area, turn east onto Antelope Flats Road from Highway 89. The view of the Tetons is splendid from here and you might also find yourself amongst a bison herd.

Above, the John Moulton Barn is often mistaken for the T.A. Moulton Barn. Courtesy NPS, photo by S. Zenner. Below, the Andy Chambers Historic District on Mormon Row features the only remaining homestead in the park. Photo courtesy the NPS.

The Gros Ventre Slide above Lower Slide Lake was one of Earth's largest land mass movements in recent history.

Gros Ventre Slide

After visiting Mormon Row, continue on Antelope Flats Road to Gros Ventre Road. Turn east on Gros Ventre Road. The road follows the Gros Ventre River and becomes Forest Road 30400 on your way up to Lower Slide Lake. This is a beautiful drive up into the Gros Ventre Mountains and quite remote. Keep your eyes peeled for bighorn sheep who frequent the area. You will see the remains of an old cabin on your left. As you travel further up the road, there is an informative pullout and photo op across from the slide that took place on Sheep Mountain forming Lower Slide Lake. To reach Lower Slide Lake, continue on the road to Atherton Creek Campground.

On July 23, 1925, rancher Guil Huff set out on horseback to investigate loud rumblings he heard in the distance. When he reached the source of the noise, he witnessed 50,000,000 cubic yards of sedimentary rock and debris sliding down the mountain towards him. He barely escaped the massive slide by only 20 feet. The slide was traveling at approximately 50 mph and continued up the opposing mountain nearly 300 feet. The debris traveled across the Gros Ventre River and formed a dam 200 feet high by 400 yards across, creating Lower Slide Lake.

The natural dam held for nearly two years and had been declared safe by scientists and engineers. On May 17, 1927, following heavy rains that melted the snowpack quicker than usual, the Gros Ventre River began spilling over the dam. The dam let loose, spilling a wall of water, boulders, trees, and debris over 50 feet tall down into the valley. The small town of Kelly at the base of the mountains was almost completely decimated and six people lost their lives to the sudden flood.

The Affair at Cunningham's Cabin

John Pierce Cunningham's cabin is the site of one of the most infamous Teton outlaw tales. Cunningham was one of the first settlers in Jackson Hole. He took out his 160-acre homestead near Spread Creek in 1885 with his wife, Margaret. The couple raised 100 head of cattle and grew hay to feed the herd. In the fall of 1892, Cunningham was approached by two strangers who were, unbeknownst to him, wanted horse thieves from Montana. The two men were in need of hay for their horses and Cunningham graciously let them stay at his ranch for the winter.

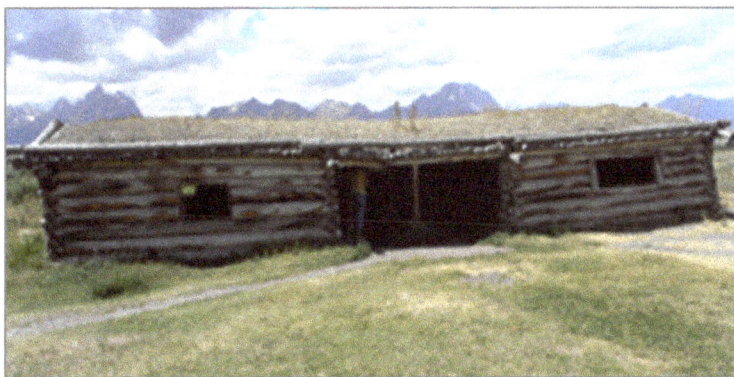

Cunningham's Cabin is one of the few original cabins remaining in the park. Photo courtesy the National Park Service.

Word of the fugitives' whereabouts made its way back to Montana. The following April, a posse formed and surrounded the cabin in the darkness of night. The horse thieves were awakened by the barking of their dogs in the early morning hours. A shootout ensued and both men were killed. The fugitives were buried in unmarked graves beside the cabin. Rumor persisted that the posse intentionally gunned down the men. They claimed this had not been there intention but supposedly two locals had been previously approached and asked to dispose of the men.

Valley residents also used Cunningham's Cabin as a fort during the Bannock Indian scare of 1895. An incident that was completely over-exaggerated into a massacre by the time it reached Eastern newspapers via telegraph. The cabin is located just off Highway 191 between the Moose and Moran Junctions. Look for a sign on the west side of the highway just north the Triangle X Ranch if you are coming from the south, and south of the Elk Ranch Flats turnout if you are coming from the north.

Lucas-Fabian and James Manges Homesteads
In 1924, Geraldine Lucas became the second woman to summit the Grand Teton. She was 58 years old. Lucas retired from a career as a school teacher and settled in Jackson Hole, south of Jenny Lake. She refused to sell her land to the Snake River Land Company, owned by John D. Rockefeller Jr. It was not until she passed away and her son sold the land to a subdivision developer that Harold Fabian, vice president of the Snake River Land Company, was able to purchase the

The Lucas-Fabian homestead at the base of the Tetons. Photo courtesy the National Park Service.

land for the future park expansion. Fabian used the cabin as a summer residence and office until 1985. The cabin and its buildings are located off of Teton Park Road just north of Teton Glacier Turnout. Look for a small, unpaved parking lot on the west side of the road then follow the walking path across Cottonwood Creek to the homestead.

The James Manges homestead is also in this vicinity. In 1911, James Manges ended William Menor's sole reign of 19 years on the west side of the Snake River when he took out his homestead near Taggart Creek. His two-story cabin is considered to be the first two-story cabin in the area. Keeping in mind the harsh Teton winters, Manges built the cabin with a sloping roof to help shed the winter's heavy snow accumulations.

Manges built guest cabins for vacationing dudes and dudines. In 1926, wealthy Californian Chester Goss purchased the Manges homestead and two neighboring homesteads. Goss built more cabins, rodeo grounds, a horse racing track, baseball field, and a general store. He called the property the Elbo Ranch and it became a very popular entertainment draw to early vacationers to Jackson Hole during the era of the dude wranglers. The Manges cabin is south of the Lucas-Fabian homestead and can be viewed from the Taggart Lake Loop Trail or across the meadow from the Cottonwood Creek picnic area just north of the Taggart Lake Trailhead parking lot off of Teton Park Road.

The Murie Center
Olaus and Margaret "Mardy" Murie were true pioneers of conservation. Their legacy and work continues today through the Murie Center. The Muries came to Jackson Hole when Olaus, a naturalist and biologist with the United States Biological Survey, was assigned to study the elk herd in 1927. They became a driving force of conservation in the valley and were an integral part of the campaign for the creation of the Jackson Hole National Monument.

The original Grand Teton National Park, created in 1929, included the Teton Range but did not encompass the lakes and valley that it does today. In 1949, John D. Rockefeller Jr. gifted 33,562 acres of land to the federal government with the express purpose that it be used for public recreation only and President Franklin Delano Roosevelt signed an executive order creating the Jackson Hole National Monument in 1949. The monument included the lakes and much of the valley along with the National Elk Refuge. On September 15, 1950, President Harry Truman signed the bill that created the Grand Teton National Park of today, minus the National Elk Refuge.

The Muries dedicated their lives to conservation in and beyond Grand Teton National Park. Olaus was the first president of the Wilderness Society, president of the Wildlife Society, and director of the Izaak Walton League. He authored several publications, including the *Peterson Field Guide to Animal Tracks*, *The Elk of North America*, and *Jackson Hole with a Naturalist*. He was also the recipient of many awards throughout his career, including the Sierra Club's John Muir Award, the Audubon Award, and the Wildlife Society's Aldo Leopold Memorial Award for outstanding publication.

Mardy was known as the Grandmother of the Conservation Movement. She was an integral part in the passage of the Wilderness Act and creation of the Arctic National Wildlife Refuge. She was a published author with works including, *Wapiti Wilderness* and *Two in the Far North*. Just before her 100th birthday, Mardy was awarded the National Wildlife Federation's highest honor of the J.N. Ding Darling Conservationist of the Year Award. Throughout her life, she was the recipient of many other awards including, the John Muir Award, Audubon Medal, and the Presidential Medal of Freedom in 1998.

The ranch where the Muries lived in Jackson Hole is now home to The Murie Center, a conservation institute. Their cabin houses the Murie Center Archives of research, photographs, personal papers, awards, art, and more. The ranch is open to researchers and the public with tours available Monday-Friday afternoons during the tourist season. Access to the Murie Center Archives is by appointment only, call (307) 739-2246. To get to the Murie Center, head south on the Moose-Wilson Road for approximately 100 yards then turn left on Murie Ranch Road. Follow the left fork in the road to park next to the center.

Laurance S. Rockefeller Preserve
When John D. Rockefeller Jr. donated over 33,000 acres of land to the United States government to expand Grand Teton National Park, he retained approximately 1,100 acres that his family used as a summer retreat for almost 70 years. The land included the former JY Ranch and was located on the shores of Phelps Lake. Following in his father's footsteps as a champion for preservation, Laurance S.

Rockefeller became known as Mr. Conservation through his roles as advisor to five presidents and chairman of the Outdoor Recreation Resource Review Commission.

Laurance restored the land to its natural state by removing the JY Ranch cabins and roads crossing the property. Over eight miles of trails were constructed along with a 7,500 square foot visitor center at an estimated cost of over $20 million. The trail network takes visitors through the meadows to Lake Creek and beautiful Phelps Lake at the base of the Tetons. The total value of the property is estimated at $160 million, making it one of the largest donations in the history of the national park system.

The visitor center is open from approximately May 31 to late September. Exhibits inside educate the public on Mr. Rockefeller's vision for the Preserve and his family's legacy of conservation for all Americans to enjoy for future generations. The Preserve is located four miles south on the east side of the Moose-Wilson Road. Call (307) 739-3654 for operating hours while you are in the park. Even if the visitor center is not open, you can still access the network of trails. Be alert for bears! When we were there in the fall, the bears were feasting on berries in the Preserve as evidenced by an abundance of berry-laced bear scat on the trails.

Colter Bay Visitor Center and Indian Arts Museum
In 1972, Laurance S. Rockefeller donated the David T. Vernon Collection of North American Indian artifacts to Grand Teton National Park. A portion of this collection is on display at Colter Bay. The collection contains 1,416 pieces of Native American artifacts, including tools, weapons, clothing, jewelry, beadwork, and art. During the summer months, Native American artists can be found in the lower level of the museum holding demonstrations and selling their artwork. In 2012, vulnerable pieces that had been restored at the Western Archeological and Conservation Center in Tucson, Arizona were returned to the Indian Arts Museum. These renovated pieces were placed on display at the Indian Arts Museum and the Craig Thomas Discovery Center. Over 1,000 artifacts are awaiting restoration in Tucson and will be returned to the museum in Grand Teton National Park.

In addition to the Indian Arts Museum, Colter Bay has a large gift shop and marina. Boat rentals are available and Jackson Lake

Cruises depart from here. There are ranger led hikes and numerous educational programs, including tipi demonstrations, wildlife watches, and park highlight programs. The center is located 25 miles north of Moose on Highway 89. Operations during the summer season are from early to mid-May through mid-October. Call (307) 739-3594 to confirm hours of operation.

Grassy Lake Road
Grassy Lake Road is located just north of Grand Teton National Park off of the John D. Rockefeller Jr. Memorial Parkway. To access the road, turn west off of the parkway at the Headwaters Lodge at Flagg Ranch. Take the first right as you approach the lodge. The initial start of this drive is paved but it soon turns to gravel and can be quite rutted. If you plan on traveling very far up the road, you will probably need a high clearance, 4-wheel drive vehicle. We made it as far as Polecat Creek, which is not too far up the road, in our Park Avenue for a little fly fishing. We could not have gone any further and in some years might not have made it that far.

View towards the Snake River at Polecat Creek on Grassy Lake Road.

The road starts out following the Snake River. When you reach the serene Polecat Creek, look upstream where you will be treated to beautiful views of the valley. It is just south of here that the Snake River flows into Jackson Lake. Continuing up the road from here will take you to Grassy Lake Reservoir and Lake of the Woods. There are 20 primitive campsites along the Grassy Lake Road that are free of charge on a first come/first serve basis. You can follow the road all the way into Idaho provided you have the proper vehicle. This is the shortest route across the Tetons into Idaho at only 12 miles but do not be fooled, it will probably take at least three hours along a very rough and rutted road through the Jedediah Smith Wilderness and Caribou-Targhee National Forest. Just think of what you might see in this remote wilderness should you choose to venture farther up this road.

This is also a beautiful area to hike in. The Polecat Creek Loop hike is 2.5 miles round trip and starts across the road from the north end of the Flagg Ranch parking lot. It is a relatively flat hike through the forest and wetlands. Other hikes starting in this vicinity are the Flagg Canyon Trail and Glade Creek Trail. Catch the Flagg Canyon Trail from the Polecat Creek Loop or park your car just north of the Snake River bridge in the parking lot. The trail begins across the road and continues along the canyon rim on the west side the Snake River. This is a beautiful area and a favorite of ours for fly fishing.

If you would like to see the area where the Snake River flows into Jackson Lake take the Glade Creek Trail. The trailhead is located up Grassy Lake Road from Flagg Ranch. Look for the parking lot and trailhead marker between the 5th and 6th campsite on the south side of the road. This trail leads you through the 1988 forest burn but quickly turns into lush forest. You will cross the footbridge over Glade Creek and continue on to where the Snake River meets Jackson Lake. This is a favorite hike for birdwatchers looking for sandhill cranes, eagles, osprey and more. Other trailheads located farther up Grassy Lake Road in the Caribou-Targhee National Forest are Cascade Creek, Union Falls, and Beula Lake. These trails are in a very remote area and a fantastic opportunity to get away from people in the park.

Interesting Fact: Today, Grassy Lake Road is also known as the Ashton-Flagg Ranch Road. In the 1800s, it was known as the Reclamation Road and Ashton Freight Road. This route was once used by early settlers in Jackson Hole to bring in supplies from Ashton, Idaho. There were no railroads coming into Jackson Hole. Men known as freighters made the trip into Idaho across this route with wagons drawn by teams of horses to bring back much needed supplies. The materials that were used to build the Jackson Lake Dam were brought into Jackson Hole in this manner.

National Elk Refuge
The National Elk Refuge was established in 1912 to provide a place of refuge for the dwindling elk herd who migrated south from Yellowstone National Park through Jackson Hole. Starting out with only 1,760 acres of land, the refuge sits just outside of Grand Teton National Park and over time has grown to 24,700 acres. Early concern over the elk herd was first voiced in 1897 when then Superintendent of Yellowstone, Colonel S.B.M. Young, asked for jurisdiction south of Yellowstone to protect the elk herd from poachers when they began their migration out of the park. It was not until Stephen Leek got involved in 1910-1911 that national attention was given to the elk herd.

Leek was among the first settlers in Jackson Hole. In 1891, he took out his homestead in the South Park area. He also established a camp on the northern edge of Jackson Lake known as Leek's Camp. Some historians consider Leek's Ranch and Camp to be the first official dude ranch in Jackson Hole. Although Leek was a hunter and guide, he abhorred the indiscriminate killing of elk by tuskers.

In the 1890s through the turn of the century, the eye teeth of the elk were popular in jewelry, in particular they were used on watch fobs as badges by the Benevolent and Protective Order of Elks. To their credit, when the Elks found out about this practice, they immediately put an end to use of elk teeth on their fobs and became strong advocates for the protection of the herd. Unfortunately, this did not put an end to the tusker activity in the Tetons and Jackson Hole as catching poachers was an integral role of park rangers through the early 1900s.

By 1911, the elk herd, once 50,000 strong, had been reduced to only 10,000. This was not solely due to the tuskers. The slowly increasing influx of settlers into the valley also played a part. Settlers put up fencing around their homesteads unaware of the consequences for the elk herd. Jackson Hole was the southern migration route for the herd on their way to their winter ranges in the Big Horn Basin, Teton Valley, Green River Basin, and Red Desert. As more and more fences went up, the elk herd eventually became trapped in Jackson Hole, an area that was not large enough to sustain the entire elk herd. The herd began dying from starvation and disease. The harsh winters of 1909-1911 exacerbated the situation and dead elk carcasses littered the landscape.

Stephen Leek took pictures of the carnage with a Kodak camera gifted to him by one of his frequent hunting guests, founder of Eastman Kodak, George Eastman. Leek became known as the "Father of the Elk" as he wrote articles on their plight and sent pictures to the national media. He also went on a lecture tour to bring attention to the starving herd. As a result, Congress declared the creation of the National Elk Refuge along Flat Creek on August 10, 1912. The Refuge expanded as early settlers' homesteads were acquired. These homesteads included those of the first two settlers in Jackson Hole, John Carnes and John Holland, along with the third settler and important yet unwitting player in the formation of Grand Teton National Park, Robert E. Miller.

Today, visitors to the Elk Refuge enjoy the Jackson Hole & Greater Yellowstone Visitor Center located at 532 N. Cache Street in Jackson, on the southwest corner of the Refuge. The visitor center houses exhibits on the migration of the elk herd, creation of the refuge and its history, and wildlife viewing information. In addition to the elk, the Refuge is home to many more species of wildlife, birds, and fish, including big game and some endangered species.

During spring and summer, visitors can stroll or cycle along the western edge of the Refuge on a multi-use pathway that runs five miles long starting just north of the visitor center, continuing north to the Gros Ventre River. Maps are also available to tour the Refuge during the summer months on the Refuge Road via automobile. The best time for wildlife viewing is in the wintertime. Visitors can opt to take a sleigh ride on the refuge or a wildlife excursion trip along Refuge Road guided by a naturalist. At certain times, elk and bison hunting is permitted with a license to help manage the herd. Special permission is not needed to fish on the Refuge but you will need a Wyoming Fishing License and should familiarize yourself with any special rules and regulations for the area.

Interesting Fact: Every spring since 1968, the Jackson District Boy Scouts have helped the Refuge staff collect antlers for their annual auction. 75% of the proceeds from this auction are donated to the U.S. Fish & Wildlife Services to aid in managing the herd and habitat on the Refuge. The antler auction takes place on the weekend before Memorial Day as part of a week-long celebration known as Elkfest. Please note, it is considered poaching and is illegal for anyone else to remove antlers from the Elk Refuge.

Historic Miller Ranch

Robert E. Miller and his wife Grace played an important role in Jackson Hole history. Robert Miller was the third settler in Jackson Hole when he took out his 160 acre homestead in 1885. He is credited with bringing the first wagon into the valley over Teton Pass. He married Grace in 1893 and built a two-story house for her which still stands today on the National Elk Refuge. Shortly after their marriage, Grace took out another 160 acre homestead. Over time, they acquired more land. The Millers dug ditches to irrigate their land and became the largest cattle ranchers in the valley with a herd totaling 400-500 head when the average herd was only 32.

The future founder and president of Jackson's first bank, Robert Miller became known as "Old Twelve Percent." He brought the first mowing machine into the valley which was quite a task. The machine was completely dismantled and pulled by pack horses over Teton Pass. He sold excess hay to area ranchers at an interest rate of 12 percent. As president of Jackson's first bank, he played an integral part in acquiring land for John D. Rockefeller Jr.'s Snake River Land Company.

The Snake River Land Company was formed by Rockefeller under the pretense of a hunting and recreation club. The players interested in establishing Grand Teton National Park felt secrecy was necessary in order to prevent inflation of land values. Park expansion was also a very controversial topic in Jackson Hole as many felt government intrusion would get in the way of ranching practices. When Miller was hired to assist in the land acquisitions, he was kept in the dark on the true purpose of the Snake River Land Company as he had voiced his opposition to park expansion. He did insist that the land owners be treated fairly in these dealings and it is unclear if he had guessed the true purpose for which he was working.

Grace Miller was industrious in her own right. She platted land she had purchased in the southern part of the valley and sold lots for homes in the town of Jackson. She was very active in the community and became the first woman mayor of Jackson in 1920. She led an all-female elected town council known as the "Petticoat Government." Jackson's all female council was one of the first in the country. The Miller homestead also served as a post office at one time which was typical in the early homesteading days in Jackson Hole.

The Town of Jackson

The town of Jackson reflects the western heritage of the area. Stroll downtown to the Jackson Town Square with its elk antler arches and take in the Old West shooting reenactment held every evening, except Sundays, at 6:15 during the summer months. Town Square is located at Broadway and Cache Street. From here you can hop a stagecoach to take a tour of the town. Do a little bit of shopping and be sure to take in some of the art galleries which house some stunning photographs and paintings of the area. Step back in time at the Jackson Hole Historical Society and Museum located at 225 N. Cache Street. Young and old will enjoy the Ripley's Believe It or Not exhibits at 140 N. Cache.

Pick a restaurant for lunch or dinner, or stop in the famous Million Dollar Cowboy Bar across from the town square. Just up the road at 105 Mercill Avenue, in the historic Coey cabin, is the new Mercill Archaeology Center housing hands on exhibits in archaeology, the fur trade, homesteading, mining, and more. The kids will enjoy (and you might, too) an afternoon on the alpine slide at Snow King Mountain Resort. Snow King also offers horseback riding, hiking and biking trails, and paragliding. Visit www.jacksonholenet.com/activities/ for a comprehensive list of things to do in and around the town of Jackson.

Mountain Climbing

If you are one of those courageous souls who longs to conquer the Grand Teton, August is the optimum time for mountain climbing. Even if you are not an experienced climber, the entire family can take lessons from the professionals at Exum Guide Service and School of Mountaineering, located at south Jenny Lake. Once you have your training, you can go on a variety of guided day climbs ranging from easy to difficult, with the ultimate being a guided climb to the summit of Grand Teton. Custom climbs and a family climbing day are available, as well as group climbs to the summit of the Grand Teton. During the winter months, the service offers guided backcountry skiing expeditions. Visit the Exum Guide website at **exumguides.com** or call (307) 733-2297 for more information.

Go Horseback Riding or Take a Pack Trip

Get a taste of frontier life from the saddle as you ride your horse along the beautiful trails in Grand Teton National Park. This relaxing family activity can be booked at most lodges in the park. Some lodges and dude ranches offer overnight pack trips into the Teton wilderness. Trips range from 1-7 days. The Triangle X, Hatchett Resort, Heart Six Guest Ranch, and Turpin Meadow Ranch are among those offering pack trips. You can even take the Teton Covered Wagon Train on a four day trip encircling the Teton Range and trailing the wilderness areas between Grand Teton and Yellowstone National Parks. You can take off on horseback to places the wagon cannot access to get deeper into the wilderness. For more information on the Teton Wagon Train and Horse Adventure visit their website at www.tetonwagontrain.com or call (888) 734-6101.

White Water Rafting

The adventurous at heart will enjoy white water rafting through the Snake River Canyon. This eight mile stretch of white water begins southwest of Jackson Hole between Hoback Junction and Alpine, Wyoming. The canyon was formed by the Snake River cutting between the Wyoming and Snake River Mountain Ranges. Rafters will be thrilled with Class II and III rapids as you plunge through the canyon over the Big Kahuna and Lunch Counter rapids. Calmer portions of the river offer ample photographic opportunities and wildlife viewing.

This is a fun activity that the entire family can enjoy, even younger children. The minimum age for children varies depending on the company so call ahead. Families with children or those not looking for a harrowing ride should choose to ride on a larger raft. The smaller the raft, the more extreme the experience. If you have the "kahunas," go for the smaller raft. The ride takes approximately 3 1/2 to 4 hours depending on where the rafting company's office is located. Some companies offer a combined white water rafting and dinner cookout. There are several companies offering white water rafting. If you are staying in Grand Teton National Park, I would recommend Lewis & Clark River Expeditions located near the Jackson Town Square at 335 N. Cache. For more information, visit their website at www.lewisandclarkriverrafting.com or call 1-800-824-5375.

Schwabacher's Landing on the Snake River. Photo courtesy the National Park Service.

Schwabacher's Landing

Some of the most stunning views and photo opportunities can be found at Schwabacher's Landing. Located on a portion of the Snake River where the terrain has flattened to grassland and forest, the still waters of the Snake provide beautiful reflections of the Teton Range. There is an easy 4 mile hike that wanders along the banks of the Snake River. Keep your eyes open for abundant wildlife. Beaver dams, river otters, bald eagles and more frequent this stretch of the river. Look for Schwabacher's Landing Road off Highway 89 approximately 5 miles north of the Moose entrance. Follow the road down to the parking lot and enjoy!

Photography Excursion

You will be in one of the most photographed areas of the world with ample opportunities to photograph gorgeous mountain landscapes, sunrise and sunsets, wildlife, and remnants of the Old West. If you want to learn how to take the best pictures possible in this unique area, a photography excursion is for you. Novice and experienced photographers will benefit from the guidance and expertise of professional photographers in the area. Photography safaris range from half or full day trips to multiple day excursions. Many services offer custom trips for your specific locations and needs. The Teton night sky is loaded with stars and night photography safaris are also available. Pricing ranges from approximately $425 for a half-day tour to $950 for a full-day tour. Below is a list of several companies offering these tours.

The Hole Picture
Website: www.the-hole-picture.com
Phone: (208) 709-3250 or (208) 483-2420

Jackson Hole Wildlife Safaris
Website: www.jacksonholewildlifesafaris.com
Phone: (307) 690-6402

AlpenGlow Tours
Website: www.alpenglowtours.com
Phone: (307) 739-1914

VIP Adventure Travel
Website: www.vipadventuretravel.com
Phone: (307) 699-1077

Wildlife Excursion

Grand Teton National Park is one of the best places in America for viewing a wide variety of wildlife. Multiple species call the park home, including grizzly bears, elk, moose, black bears, antelope, bison, wolves, foxes, bighorn sheep, and more. Although you may be able to drive through the park and spot many species, guides on the wildlife excursions will have a better knowledge of where to find different species at certain times of the year. You can book a wildlife excursion through many resorts in the park and through the companies listed below.

Wildlife Expeditions of Teton Science Schools
Website: www.tetonscience.org/wildlife-expeditions/home/
Phone: (877) 404-6626

EcoTour Adventures
Website: www.jhecotouradventures.com
Phone: (307) 690-9533

Jackson Hole Wildlife Safaris
Website: www.jacksonholewildlifesafaris.com
Phone: (307) 690-6402

AlpenGlow Tours
Website: www.alpenglowtours.com
Phone: (307) 739-1914

VIP Adventure Travel
Website: www.vipadventuretravel.com
Phone: (307) 699-1077

Grizzly Country Wildlife Adventures
Website: www.grizzlycountrywildlifeadventures.com
Phone: (307) 413-4389

Scenic Safaris
Website: www.scenic-safaris.com
Phone: (888) 734-8898

Four

HIKE INTO THE WILDERNESS

With over 200 miles of trails there are many hikes to be enjoyed in Grand Teton National Park, no matter what your fitness level. Best of all, you do not have to be a mountain climber to enjoy the beautiful vistas, canyons, and waterfalls in the park. Know and adhere to your own physical conditioning. Pushing your limits too far can result in injuries and the need for rescue personnel. This is by no means an all-inclusive list of the trails within Grand Teton National Park. There are many more and several of the trails have off-shoot loops taking you to an additional lake or hidden mountain treasure. If you love to hike, buy yourself a book on the trails in the park. Most hiking books have graded the trails according to difficulty level so all can enjoy the splendor of Grand Teton National Park.

Be Prepared
Weather can and does change rapidly in the mountains. Take along extra clothing when hiking into the higher elevations, wear sunscreen, and take plenty of water and high energy snacks. If you are planning a long hike, start in the morning and keep your eye on the time. You do not want to be caught on the trail after dark.

Be Bear Aware
You will notice these signs everywhere in the park. Take them seriously. At certain times of the year, some trails may be closed due to increased bear activity. Park rangers put on bear safety presentations which you should consider attending. Whenever you are hiking in the park always take along bear spray, know how to use it, have it immediately available, and talk or make noise while you hike. Never hike alone.

Backcountry Camping and Mountain Climbing
All overnight stays in the backcountry require a permit. Permits are allotted on a first-come, first-serve basis no more than one day in advance of your stay. Permits are available at the Colter Bay Visitor Center, Jenny Lake Ranger Station, and the Craig Thomas Discovery and Visitor Center. Advance reservations can be made online beginning at some point in January through mid-May but only 1/3 of the permits are allotted for advance reservations. Mountain climbing permits are not required unless your climb involves an overnight stay. Permits for overnight stays while mountain climbing must be obtained through the Jenny Lake Ranger Station.

Take along a compass or satellite GPS device for backcountry navigation. Do not count on your cell phone for navigation in the park. There are many places where you cannot receive a signal. If you have a GPS app on your phone, it may not work unless you have a data connection. You cannot count on your cell phone to get a signal for data or to make a call should you get lost.

Backpackers are required to carry park approved bear resistant food canisters while in the backcountry except in locations where food storage boxes have been provided. The park service provides bear resistant canisters free of charge. Know the regulations for backpacking in Grand Teton National Park before you go. Download the National Park Service Backcountry Camping Guide here: www.nps.gov/grte/planyourvisit/upload/Backcountry13_web.pdf.

Easy Hikes with Big Rewards

Do not be fooled by the easy rating on these hikes. Just because they have an easy rating does not mean they are any less beautiful than the longer more strenuous hikes in the park. You will enjoy beautiful mountain lakes, meadows, and waterfalls. My top recommendation if you are only going to do one hike during your stay is the Hidden Falls/Inspiration Point Hike via the Jenny Lake boat shuttle.

Hidden Falls and Inspiration Point Hike via Jenny Lake Boat Dock
If you are not up for the 7.7 mile loop around Jenny Lake, take the boat from the South Jenny Lake parking lot. The boat departs approximately every 15 minutes and is a beautiful ride across the lake. Once you disembark, it is only a 0.2 mile hike to Hidden Falls and another 0.4 miles on to Inspiration Point where you'll enjoy sweeping vistas of Jenny Lake and the valley below. This is a gradual but simple climb on a well-traveled trail. If you are afraid of heights, you may not be able to complete the last section of trail up to Inspiration Point as the trail is on the side of a rock wall although the drop-off is not as high as it seems. Looking out over the valley makes you feel like you are way up in the air. There is a very nice lookout point just before this last bit of trail so you can still enjoy the view from up here.

Lakeshore Trail Hike at Colter Bay, Jackson Lake
This flat, 2.0 mile loop trail follows the shoreline along a peninsula in Colter Bay. You will enjoy beautiful views of Mount Moran across Jackson Lake and reflections in Colter Bay. The trail begins on a paved service road near the boat docks at the Colter Bay Marina.

Heron Pond and Swan Lake Hike
If you enjoy waterfowl, wildlife, and water lily covered ponds, this hike is for you. Look for trumpeter swans, beaver, moose, and bears. This relatively flat hike starts at Colter Bay Village and is a 3.0 mile loop.

Willow Flats Shuttle or Loop Hike
When snow still covers the mountain trails in the spring, the Willow Flats area west of Jackson Lake will be snow free and ready for hiking. The willows and marshes are prime habitat for a variety of wildlife. Look for moose, sandhill cranes, beaver, bears, and other wildlife. The

area is, as the name suggests, flat and it can get rather warm trekking through the flats and open meadows due to the lack of shade trees so you may want to choose a cooler day for this hike.

The shuttle hike is 4.9 miles. You can start the shuttle hike from either the Colter Bay coral or at the small parking lot on the south side of Jackson Lake Lodge. For the shuttle, you will need to park your car at either end and get a ride back to the trailhead. The loop trail is 8.3 miles starting at the Jackson Lake Lodge trailhead. The shuttle and first part of the loop trail are actually an abandoned dirt service road.

String Lake Hike
Nestled between Jenny Lake and Leigh Lake, what String Lake lacks in size it makes up for in beauty. This relatively flat 3.4 mile loop hike is wheelchair accessible for approximately 0.3 miles and we maneuvered a sturdy stroller through the entire hike with an occasional lift by Mom and Dad. You'll enjoy beautiful mountain views reflecting in a placid lake, footbridges, and streams. Begin your hike at the String Lake Trailhead parking lot by turning west at the North Jenny Lake Junction turnoff from Teton Park Road.

Leigh Lake Hike
This beautiful hike starts at the String Lake Trailhead and is 5.6 miles round trip. It follows String Lake before veering off into a lodgepole pine forest and on through open meadows before revealing the isolated splendor of Leigh Lake in about a mile. It is a good choice for hiking in the spring when the higher elevation trails are still snow covered. Mount Moran towers over the lake and you can see into Paintbrush and Leigh Canyons as you hike along the lakeshore.

Taggart Lake Hike
I absolutely love this 4.0 mile loop hike. Park your car at the Taggart Lake Trailhead parking lot (off Teton Park Road) and follow the path to your right (north). You will soon be crossing the footbridge over Taggart Creek, the perfect spot for your first picture. I cannot exactly call this hike easy as it is a gradual uphill climb to Taggart Lake. You may need to make a few pit stops to catch your breath but continue on. You will be rewarded with splendid views of the Grand Teton over the lake. Once you cross the footbridge at the outlet of the lake there is a little bit more of a climb but the rest is all downhill. Be sure to turn around to catch the view overlooking Taggart Lake.

Moderate Hikes

This collection of moderate hikes gets its rating either because there are some short, steep sections on the trail or they are a longer distance which may test some people's endurance. When planning your hikes, remember that you will cover approximately 2 miles per hour and should add an extra hour to the time necessary to complete the hike for every 1,000 feet of elevation gain.

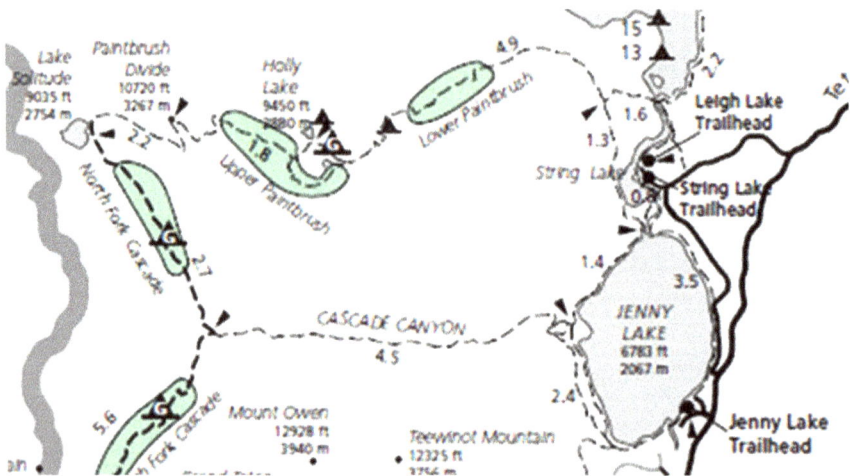

Map for the Jenny Lake and Cascade Canyon Hikes courtesy NPS.

Jenny Lake

Some consider Jenny Lake to be the most picturesque lake in the park, and it is gorgeous. This 7.3 mile loop takes you all the way around the shoreline of Jenny Lake. Start your hike by parking in either the String Lake Trailhead parking lot or the parking lot at the South Jenny Lake Junction off of Teton Park Road. I recommend starting at the String Lake Trailhead in the morning. This way you will be arriving at the south end of Jenny Lake around lunch time where you can grab a bite to eat, enjoy the visitor center, and use the facilities before completing your hike. A worthy side trip while on this hike is the loop up to Hidden Falls and Inspiration Point.

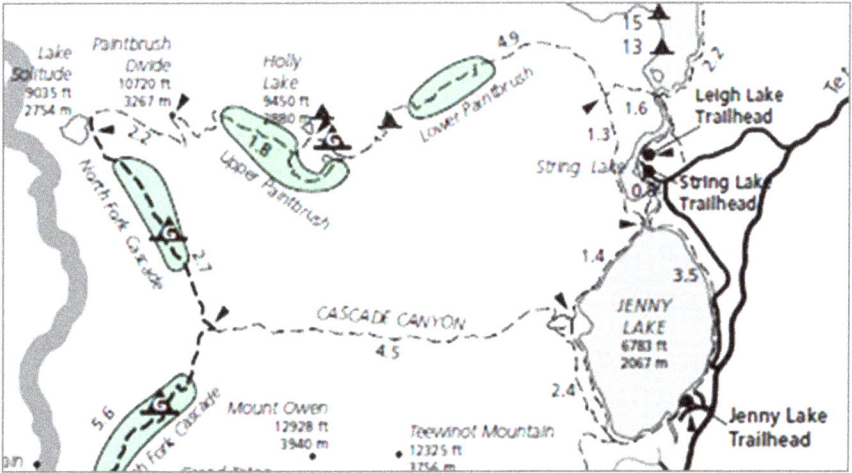

Map for the Jenny Lake and Cascade Canyon Hikes courtesy NPS.

Cascade Canyon via Jenny Lake Boat Dock

The Cascade Canyon hike continues on past Hidden Falls and Inspiration Point. This the perfect opportunity to get into the back country with mountains soaring above you on either side. After leaving Inspiration Point, the trail climbs steeply for about a mile but once you get past this it becomes a gradual climb through the meadows of the canyon. You will hear and see crystal clear Cascade Creek roaring through the canyon to Hidden Falls below. The trail is 9.8 miles round trip if you go all the way to the junction with the Lake Solitude and Paintbrush Canyon trails. If you are planning to take the boat back across Jenny Lake on your return be sure to check the last departure time before you leave. If you miss the boat you can follow the Jenny Lake Trail an additional 2.1 miles back to the parking lot. Due to the higher elevation of this climb and lingering snow, the best months to complete the hike are July and August. Check with a park ranger for trail conditions.

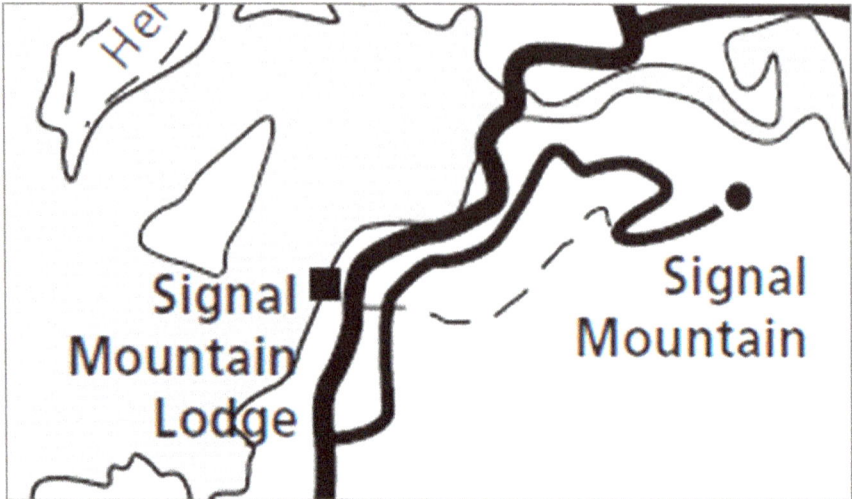

Map for Signal Mountain Summit trail courtesy NPS.

Signal Mountain Summit

Park your car at the Signal Mountain Lodge parking lot and catch the trailhead from there. The hike to the summit is 3.7 miles one way and has some moderately steep inclines along the way. If you are hiking in spring, be sure to inquire about the condition of the trail before you start your hike. The trail can be snow covered and muddy into early summer. If you choose to hike the trail, you will be rewarded with some bonuses you will not have access to if you drive to the top. The trail passes along the shore of a small lake, before plunging back into the forest. You will pass through meadows and along streams. The trail gets rockier the further up you go and ends with a series of switchbacks before reaching the summit. Retrace your steps back down to Signal Mountain Lodge and satisfy the appetite you have worked up at the Trapper Grill.

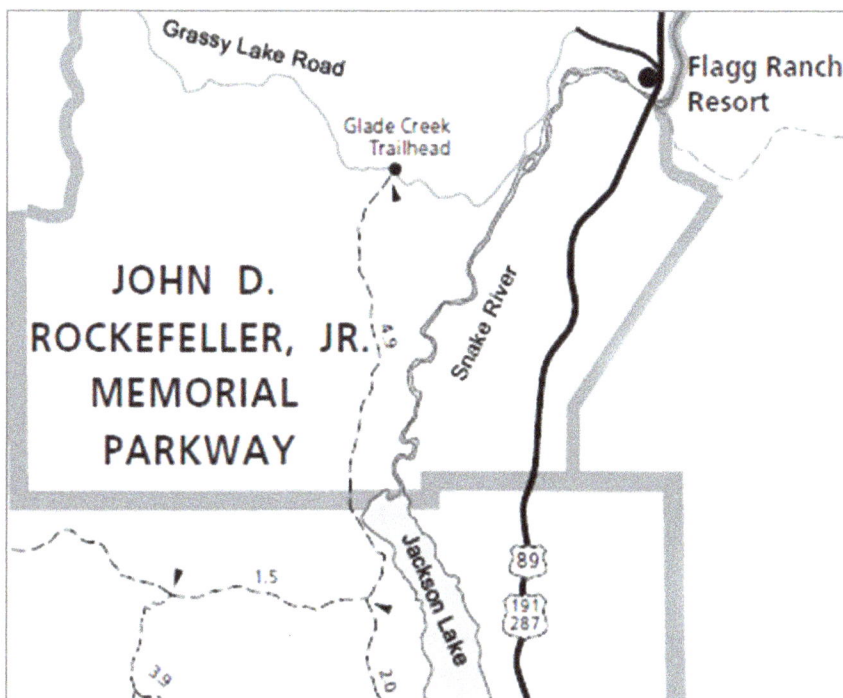

Map for Glade Creek Trail courtesy National Park Service.

Glade Creek

Glade Creek lies in the northernmost portion of Grand Teton National Park. This area of the park does not get near the traffic as the rest of the park so you will likely have the Glade Creek Trail to yourself. To get to the trailhead drive north on John D. Rockefeller Jr. Memorial Parkway to Flagg Ranch. Go west on Grassy Lake Road for almost 4.5 miles. The trailhead will be on the south side of the road. The trail begins in a lodgepole pine forest. After crossing the footbridge over Glade Creek, you will drop down into a meadow and follow the Snake River as it flows towards Jackson Lake. The meadow turns into a large freshwater marsh which hosts a multitude of wildlife. Be on the lookout for moose in their favorite habitat. The trail is 7 miles round trip and you will want to bring mosquito spray for the marsh area. The terrain is relatively flat and rated as a moderate hike for its distance. The Glade Creek Trail is also the starting point for the Berry Creek, Owl Canyon, and Webb Canyon trails into the backcountry, requiring overnight stays.

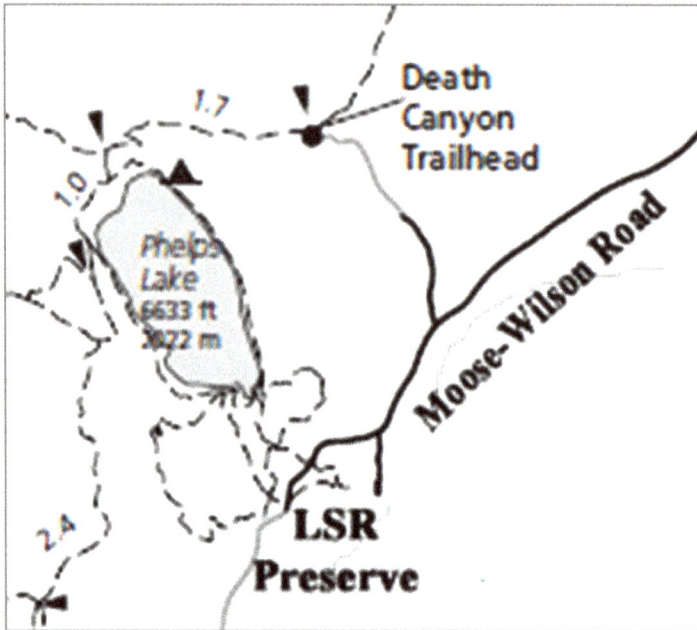

Map for Phelps Lake hike courtesy National Park Service.

Phelps Lake

When John D. Rockefeller Jr. gifted over 33,000 acres of land for the creation of Grand Teton National Park, he retained property for a family retreat on beautiful Phelps Lake. You can hike to Phelps Lake from many different trails, including from the Laurance S. Rockefeller Preserve, but the shortest route begins at the Death Canyon Trailhead. To get to the trailhead follow the Moose-Wilson Road 3.1 miles south. Turn west at the Death Canyon Trailhead turnout and follow the road to the trailhead, 1.6 miles. Start on the Death Canyon Trail and keep southwest at the first junction. You are now on the Valley Trail which takes you to the Phelps Lake Overlook then follows the west side of the lake. There is a steep switchback that you go down on your way to Phelps Lake which does result in a fairly steep climb on your return hike. The total distance of the hike is 4 miles. The area is well known for moose and black bears. In recent years, grizzly bears have also started frequenting this area of the park.

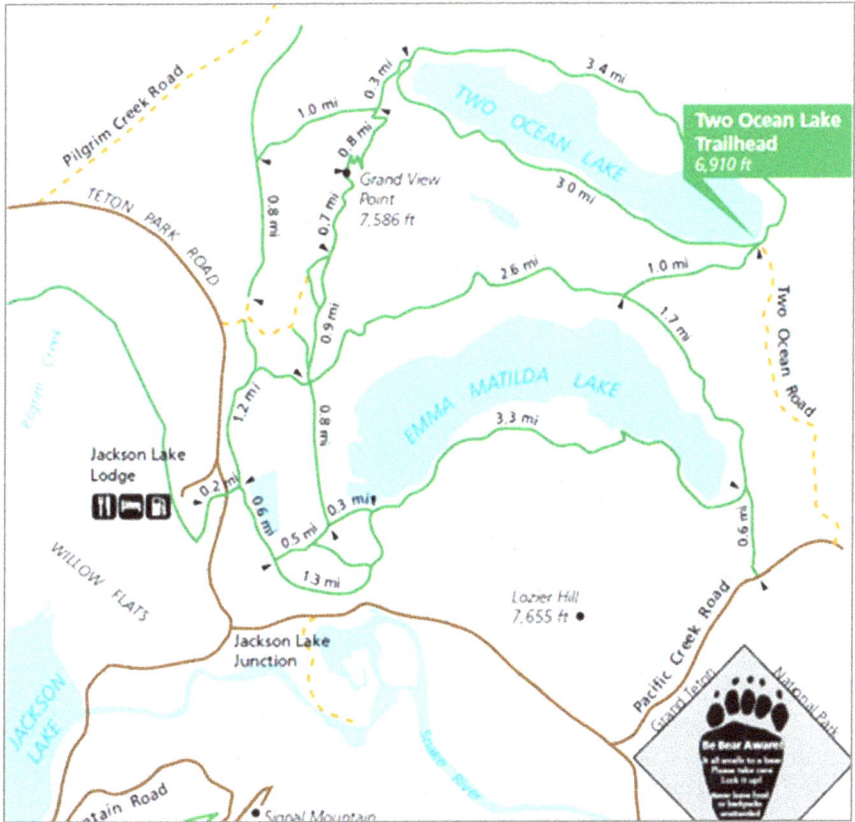

Map for Grand View Point, Two Ocean Lake, and Emma Matilda Lake Trails courtesy National Park Service.

Grand View Point

Some may classify this hike as easy due to its short distance of 2.2 miles. However, in order to enjoy the spectacular view that this hike rewards, you must climb a steep hill. People with certain health or physical issues may find this quite difficult. That being said, the view of Mount Moran and the Tetons to the west, and Two Ocean Lake to the northeast, make the steep climb well worth the effort. The trailhead is located 0.8 miles up a high clearance road. If you don't have a high clearance vehicle, park at the bottom of the road and hike from there. This access road is the first right (east) turn north of the Jackson Lake Lodge turnout, approximately one mile north of the lodge. While you are here, consider continuing on the trail another 1.3 miles for a close up view of Two Ocean Lake before you return. If you have the stamina, you can hike the 6.4 mile loop around Two Ocean Lake from here. You can also make a different loop out of this trip by heading west on the Pilgrim Creek Trail 0.9 miles further north up the trail from Grand View Point for a total distance of 4.4 miles back to your vehicle. Note: Two Ocean Lake is sometimes closed due to increased grizzly bear activity. Check with a park ranger first if you are planning on hiking around the lake, always make noise when hiking, and have your bear spray readily accessible.

Two Ocean Lake
Many people mistakenly believe that Two Ocean Lake is the starting point for two creeks, one that flows to the Atlantic Ocean and another that flows to the Pacific Ocean. The lake is actually named after Two Ocean Pass to the northeast where Atlantic Creek flows to the Atlantic Ocean and Pacific Creek flows to the Pacific Ocean. Two Ocean Lake flows into Pacific Creek only. The trailhead is located at the top of Two Ocean Lake Road. Drive 2.6 miles east of the Jackson Lake Junction on Highway 287 or 1.2 miles west of the Moran Junction then turn north onto Pacific Creek Road. Follow Pacific Creek Road for 2 miles then turn left onto Two Ocean Lake Road and follow to the picnic area and trailhead. The loop around the lake is 6.4 miles round trip. The north shore provides the best views of the lake with the Tetons in the background. Be on the lookout for wildlife and waterfowl as you hike. If you are not going to hike to Grand View Point on a different occasion, consider taking the trail at the west end of the lake for 1.3 miles to the point. Note: Two Ocean Lake is sometimes closed due to increased grizzly bear activity. It can also be closed in the spring due to poor road conditions from the melting snow. Check with a park ranger first if you are planning on hiking around the lake, always make noise when hiking, and have your bear spray readily accessible.

Emma Matilda Lake
Emma Matilda Lake can be reached via a trail from the Two Ocean Lake Trailhead or you can park your car 2 miles up Pacific Creek Road at the Emma Matilda Lake pullout. The lake is named after William Owen's wife. Owen was one of four men to make the first documented ascent of the Grand Teton in 1898. The trail around the lake is fairly easy but it is an 11.8 mile loop which gets it a moderate

rating. The trail follows the northern side of the lake and winds through a pine forest leading to a lookout point with inspiring views of the lake, the Teton Range, Jackson Lake, and Christian Pond. On the south side of the lake, the trail goes through dense forest with fewer lake views. Note: Emma Matilda Lake is sometimes closed due to increased grizzly bear activity. Check with a park ranger first if you are planning on hiking around the lake, always make noise when hiking, and have your bear spray readily accessible.

Five

VENTURE INTO THE BACKCOUNTRY

Backcountry hiking offers the special reward of really getting into the wilderness and seeing fewer people. Most of these backcountry hikes are a longer distance and may require overnight stays to complete. Some also require mountain climbing skills to traverse sections of the trail. Know your skill set, backcountry regulations, and be sure to obtain a backcountry permit before you depart. This is a good time to ask a park ranger if there is special experience required for the trail you are hiking. Be prepared for any type of weather in the upper elevations of the park no matter the month. Trails in the higher elevations may be covered with snow into August. When planning your backcountry trip allow for a speed of no more than 2 miles per hour and an additional hour for every 1,000 feet of elevation gain.

The backcountry is home to grizzly bears and other large wildlife species. I know I have said this repeatedly throughout the book but it bears repeating (no pun intended) - Be Bear Aware. Have your bear spray readily available and avoid an encounter by never hiking alone and making noise. If you do encounter a bear do not run as this may incite the bear to pick up the chase. Slowly retreat, downwind if possible. If the bear has noticed you, do not make eye contact while retreating. Should the bear decide to charge, park rangers recommend staying still. Many times a bear will bluff charge and stop before actually attacking. If this happens, use your bear spray and retreat. If you are being attacked by a bear, lay flat on your stomach and cover the back of your neck for protection. Remain still until you are sure the bear has left the area.

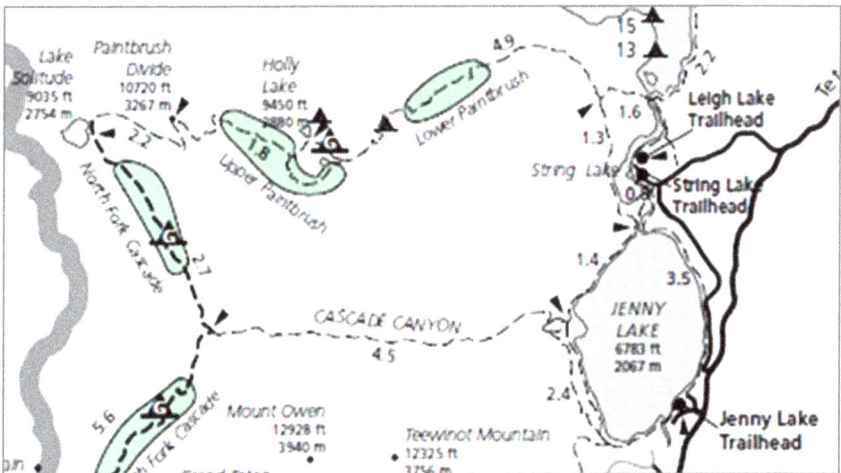

Map for Paintbrush Canyon to Cascade Canyon Loop courtesy National Park Service. Green areas represent camping sites.

Paintbrush Canyon, Lake Solitude, Cascade Canyon Loop

This 19.2 mile hike starting at the String Lake Trailhead is often billed as the prettiest hike in the park for good reason. You will be ascending through rugged canyons and forests, past mountain lakes and alpine meadows, to Paintbrush Divide at 10,720 feet. The Teton peaks will shepherd the way with stunning views you will not see from the valley floor below. To get started, park your car in the String Lake Picnic Area parking lot. Take the String Lake Trail across the footbridge between Jenny and String Lakes. You will come to a Y in the trail in 0.2 miles, follow the trail to the right towards Paintbrush Canyon. This portion of the trail changes from woodlands to grasslands before opening onto hillsides dotted with boulders. Cross through the aspen grove and over a creek before veering left at the next Y in the trail. Here you will start your ascent into Paintbrush Canyon. Large boulder fields flank the trail and the trail itself gradually becomes rockier. Be on the lookout for waterfalls and Lake of the Crags (to your left) as you ascend through the canyon. When you reach the first camping area, you will be rewarded with breathtaking valley views.

Shortly after this campsite, the trail turns into a series of steep switchbacks through debris fields. At the next Y junction, veer to the right for a side trip to Holly Lake. Return to the main trail from Holly Lake. You are now in the second camping area before crossing Paintbrush Divide. You may choose to camp here or continue on over the divide past Lake Solitude (be sure to take the short side trail to the lake) on the Lake Solitude/North Fork Cascade Canyon Trail where you can camp in the shadow of the Grand Teton, Mount Owen, and Teewinot Mountain.

The Cascade Canyon Trail is 2.7 miles down the trail. Take a left at the junction to continue down Cascade Canyon towards Jenny Lake. You only have another 4.5 miles to go to Inspiration Point overlooking Jenny Lake and the valley of Jackson Hole. After passing through a pine forest, the trail opens up again in Cascade Canyon. This is one of the most stunning views in the park with jagged mountains towering over you on both sides as you make your descent. Listen for Cascade Creek serenading you as it tumbles its way down to Hidden Falls and Jenny Lake. When you reach Jenny Lake, turn left on the trail to hike 1.4 miles northeast back to the parking lot. If you have already been to Inspiration Point, when you come to the Y in the trail take the left fork and follow around to the parking lot. The right fork will take you to Inspiration Point.

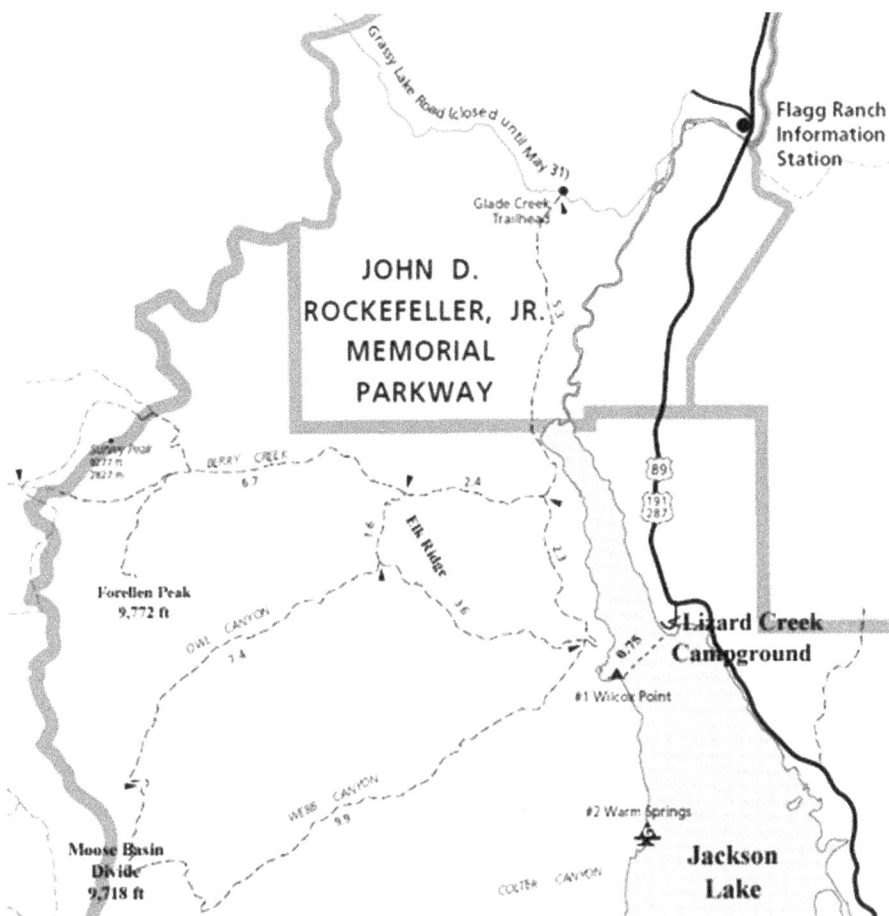

Map for Berry Creek and Owl Canyon-Webb Canyon Loop trails courtesy National Park Service.

Berry Creek and Owl Canyon-Webb Canyon Loop

The Berry Creek Trail and the Owl Canyon-Webb Canyon Loop can both be accessed via the Glade Creek Trail. You can cut miles off of these hikes by renting a canoe at the Colter Bay Marina. Park your car at the Lizard Creek Campground and launch your canoe from there. It is approximately a 0.75 mile paddle across Jackson Lake to Wilcox Point. The trail begins just north of the backcountry patrol cabin at Wilcox Point. Paddling across Jackson Lake will save you 5.3 miles on the way to the Berry Creek Trail. It will save you 7.6 miles if you are hiking the Owl Canyon-Webb Canyon Loop. Note: Grassy Lake Road is closed until May 31st due to grizzly bear activity. The canyons, creeks, and forests of this section of the park are prime grizzly bear habitat. Plan accordingly if you are going to start at the Glade Creek Trailhead.

Berry Creek Trail to Survey Peak and Forellen Peak
The Berry Creek Trail runs approximately 14.4 miles out to either Survey or Forellen Peaks starting from the Glade Creek Trailhead located on Grassy Lake Road. If you launch a canoe at the Lizard Creek Campground and paddle across Jackson Lake to Wilcox Point, you can follow the trail north along the lake for 2.3 miles to the intersection with the Berry Creek Trail where you turn west for a total of 11.4 miles out. Alternatively, you can hike 3.6 miles west on the Owl Canyon Trail. Here a 1.6 mile trail links north above Elk Ridge to the Berry Creek Trail for a total of 11.9 miles out. If you have started at Wilcox Point, take one way up and another way back to see more of the backcountry. The Berry Creek Trail crosses streams without footbridges. This can be dangerous, especially in spring when the streams are running high with snow melt. Hiking can be strenuous towards either peak yet nontechnical and includes low maintenance trails and off-trail hiking.

Owl Canyon-Webb Canyon Loop Crossing the Moose Basin Divide
If you paddle across Jackson Lake, the Owl Canyon-Webb Canyon loop is 20.9 miles. Starting at the Glade Creek Trailhead will add another 15.2 miles roundtrip. If you take the Glade Creek Trail, follow it south for 7.6 miles then turn west on the Berry Creek Trail to head up Owl Canyon. From Wilcox Point the Berry Creek Trail is located just north of the patrol cabin. For the most part, the trail follows Berry Creek to the confluence with Owl Creek. On your way up Owl Canyon, you will have numerous crossings of Berry and Owl Creeks with no footbridges. Proceed with caution, the water can be as high as waist deep in the spring snow melt. As you reach the confluence, look toward Forellen Peak. From here you can see the Forellean Fault crossing over the peak, dividing the northern limestone from the southern granite. You may even spot some bighorn sheep. Depending on your starting point, you may choose to camp here for the night. It is over 7 miles from here to the Moose Basin Divide. The trail runs alongside Owl Creek up to the divide. While the beginning of the hike

is a more gradual climb, the last few miles to the divide climb over 2,500 feet.

Spend the night in the Moose Basin or take an extra day to explore this remote subalpine region of the park. Once you cross the divide, you start descending through Webb Canyon. The trail follows Moose Creek as it rushes downward through the canyon and yes, you will have to get your feet wet crossing the stream several more times. It is nearly 10 miles down Webb Canyon from the Moose Basin. You may want to plan an overnight stay on the way down.

As you near the end of Webb Canyon, look for an old mine shaft that is well hidden along the creek. Every spring and summer for 23 years, John Graul would return to his mine along Moose Creek. Over this time, he managed to cut a tunnel 193 feet long through the solid igneous rock. It is not known what he was tunneling for. Many prospectors came to the Tetons hoping to strike it rich mining for gold but no measurable quantities were ever found. Amateur archaeologist W.C. "Slim" Lawrence, who owned an asbestos claim in the Berry Creek canyon, speculated that Graul was tunneling for platinum. It remains a mystery as Graul was killed in a mining accident in Colorado before discovering anything. Enjoy the view of Jackson Lake as you near the homestretch of the trail to catch the Glade Creek Trail or paddle your way across Jackson Lake from Wilcox Point.

More Backcountry Hikes
The above hikes are just a small sampling of available backcountry trails. Other popular backcountry hikes include the Teton Crest Trail past the Death Canyon Shelf and Alaska Basin, Death Canyon Trail, Granite Canyon Trail, and more. If you are serious about hiking into the backcountry of Grand Teton National Park buy a book on this topic. You should also download the National Park Service's guide to Backcountry Camping in Grand Teton National Park at www.nps.gov/grte/planyourvisit/upload/Backcountry14.pdf.

Six

DAILY ITINERARIES

The suggested itineraries are meant to help you maximize your drive time to enjoy park destinations within the same area. The park is vast and if you are not careful you can spend a lot of time driving to different destinations. For the purpose of the daily itineraries, the assumption is being made that you are staying in or near the park, that this is your first trip to Grand Teton National Park, and that you will be staying for 5-7 days. If you are a returning visitor or on an extended stay incorporate some of the activities in Chapter 3 – Beyond the Highlights.

     With a few exceptions, most daily itineraries have a main activity that will take up most of a morning or afternoon. If possible, bring collapsible chairs when you come to the park. There are many places you will want to pull up and park, plop your chair down, enjoy the view, and wait for wildlife to make an appearance. Most importantly, take time to relax and try not to cram too many activities into one day.

Daily Itinerary #1
Highlight: Snake River Scenic Float Trip

- Snake River Scenic Float Trip

- Lunch at Signal Mountain Lodge

- Hike or drive to the Signal Mountain Summit for spectacular views of the Tetons, Jackson Lake, and the valley of Jackson Hole.

- Chapel of the Sacred Heart

- Jackson Lake Dam

- Take time along this stretch of road between the dam and Jackson Lake Junction enjoying the pullouts for wildlife viewing and beautiful photo opportunities.

- Turn north at the Jackson Lake Junction and stop at the Willow Flats Overlook. This is an excellent photo op of the Tetons rising behind Jackson Lake and prime moose habitat.

- Have an early dinner at the Jackson Lake Lodge then head over to Oxbow Bend for spectacular shots of the sun setting behind the Tetons. Bonus, as dusk approaches you may be treated to various forms of wildlife at the water's edge.

Snake River Float Trips fill up fast, make reservations through your lodge the first day you arrive.

Daily Itinerary #2
Highlight: Chuckwagon Cowboy Breakfast

- Sunrise photography at Oxbow Bend, Signal Mountain Lodge, or Willow Flats (There is nothing like the pink glow of the rising sun on the peaks of the Tetons.)

- Chuckwagon Cowboy Breakfast (Enjoy the ride to and from breakfast in the Willow Flats. Keep your eyes open for wildlife and spectacular views.)

- Wear off that wonderful breakfast by indulging in a hike. If your breakfast started at the Jackson Lake Lodge corral, nearby hikes include:
  - Willow Flats
  - Christian Pond
  - Lookout Rock
  - Grand View Point
  - Two Ocean Lake

  - If your breakfast ride started at the Colter Bay corral, nearby hikes include:
    - Heron Pond and Swan Lake
    - Lakeshore Trail
    - Hermitage Point
    - Glade Creek (A short drive north to Flagg Ranch and Grassy Lake Road.)

- Colter Bay Visitor Center & Indian Arts Museum

- Dinner at Colter Bay

- Head down to the marina at Colter Bay for stunning sunset photos after dinner.

Daily Itinerary #3
Highlight: Jenny Lake, Hidden Falls, Inspiration Point, Cascade Canyon

- After breakfast, drive the scenic loop road at Jenny Lake and take in the photo opportunities at the overlooks.

- Hop aboard the boat at the South Jenny Lake dock for a lake ride to the base of the Hidden Falls Trail. Alternatively, you can hike around Jenny Lake on the Jenny Lake Trail to the Hidden Falls Trail. If you are planning on hiking into Cascade Canyon, be sure to start this hike in the morning and keep your eye on the time so you are sure to get back to the dock before the last boat departs.

- The first destination after departing at the dock is the hike to Hidden Falls. From there, you can continue on to Inspiration Point and further into Cascade Canyon. I recommend hiking at least to Inspiration Point. This will fill up your morning.

- If you have time, Cascade Canyon is one of the most beautiful hikes in the park. If you are planning on going to Cascade Canyon, be sure and pack snacks and plenty of water. Hiking into Cascade Canyon and back will completely fill your day and you will be ready for a relaxing dinner when you return.

- If you turned around at Inspiration Point, enjoy lunch at the Jenny Lake Lodge.

- Spend the rest of the afternoon leisurely enjoying the turnouts and attractions below along a driving loop heading south on Teton Park Road and back north up Highway 89.
    - Teton Glacier Turnout
    - Windy Point Turnout
    - Murie Ranch
    - Chapel of the Transfiguration
    - Menor's Ferry Historic District
    - Craig Thomas Discovery Center (Moose Visitor Center)
    - Dornan's

- Blacktail Ponds Overlook
- Glacier View Turnout
- Schwabacher Landing (Take Schwabacher Road west off of Highway 89.)
- Teton Point Turnout
- Snake River Overlook
- Deadman's Bar (Take Deadman's Bar Road west off of Highway 89, may need a high clearance vehicle.)
- Cunningham Cabin
- Elk Ranch Flats Turnout
- Oxbow Bend Turnout
- Cattlemen's Bridge (Look for the gravel road on the south side of Highway 89, just past Oxbow Bend.)

This will bring you back to the Jackson Lake Junction. Enjoy the remaining turnouts on the way back to your lodge.

Daily Itinerary #4
Highlight: Yellowstone National Park

- After breakfast, gas up and head north to Yellowstone National Park via the John D. Rockefeller Jr. Memorial Parkway.

- Choose either the "Day Trip to Yellowstone" or the "Yellowstone Grand Loop" route from "Highlights for Your First Trip" and enjoy your visit to Yellowstone.

- If you have time, spend two days in Yellowstone.
  - Day One: Day Trip to Yellowstone
  - Day Two: Yellowstone Grand Loop (Omit Old Faithful, the Geyser Basins, and Gibbon Falls.)

Daily Itinerary #5
Highlight: Guided Fishing and
Jackson Lake Boat Cruise for Dinner

- Enjoy a guided fly fishing trip on the Snake River or a guided fishing trip on Jackson Lake in search of a monster lake trout.

- If fishing is not your thing, consider a wildlife safari or photography excursion.

- Follow this up with the Jackson Lake Boat Cruise featuring dinner on Elk Island.

These activities fill up fast, make reservations through your lodge the first day you arrive.

Daily Itinerary #6
Highlight: Moose-Wilson Road and
Tram Ride at Teton Village

- Head south on the Moose-Wilson Road. (Note: this is a slow, scenic drive.)

- Stop at the Sawmill Ponds Overlook (first overlook you come to on your left) for fantastic wildlife viewing opportunities.

- Laurance S. Rockefeller Preserve

- Go inside, enjoy the exhibits, and learn about Laurance's vision for the Preserve.

- Enjoy some time hiking the trails in the preserve for beautiful views of Phelps Lake, Death Canyon, and more.

- Continue your leisurely drive along the Moose-Wilson Road. Keep your eyes open for moose, elk, bear, and other wildlife along your drive.

- After exiting the park, continue on Moose-Wilson Road until you come to Teton Village.

- Board the tram to the top of Rendezvous Mountain for spectacular views of Jackson Hole, the Teton Range, and Gros Ventre Mountains.

- Indulge in some delicious waffles at Corbet's Cabin.

- Hike around on the trails.

- If you are feeling adventurous, you can even fly tandem and paraglide back down to the valley floor with a paragliding professional.

- After your descent, explore the many shops and restaurants at Teton Village.

Depending on how much time you spent exploring the trails, you may still have time for other activities.
- Mormon Row
- TA Moulton and John Moulton barns.
- Andy Chambers Homestead
- Gros Ventre Slide and Lower Slide Lake
- The town of Kelly. Kelly was almost completely decimated when the dam created by the Gros Ventre Slide broke loose and flooded the town in 1927. Six people lost their lives.

Daily Itinerary #7
Highlight: National Elk Refuge and the Town of Jackson

- Head south on Highway 89 or take the slower, scenic Moose-Wilson Road to the Jackson Hole & Greater Yellowstone Visitor Center at 532 N. Cache Street in Jackson. This is located on the southwest corner of the National Elk Refuge.
- National Elk Refuge
    - Enjoy the interactive displays and learn about the elk at the visitor center.
    - Walk or bike along the multi-use pathway.
    - Drive along Refuge Road. Maps are available at the visitor center.
    - If you are visiting in the winter, take a horse-drawn sleigh ride through the refuge.
    - Bring your camera for wildlife photography opportunities. In addition to the elk herd, the refuge supports many other species of wildlife, including bison, wolves, trumpeter swans, bald eagles, and more.

- Historic Miller Ranch, an early Jackson Hole homestead and the first property purchased for the National Elk Refuge. The homestead is located 3/4 mile north of the East Broadway Street entrance to the refuge.

- Jackson Hole Historical Society & Museum located at 225 N. Cache Street

- Young and old will enjoy the Ripley's Believe It or Not Museum at 140 N. Cache Street.

- Jackson Town Square at the intersection of Broadway and Cache Streets.

- Hop a stagecoach for a ride around town.

- Enjoy an Old West shootout reenactment on summer evenings.

- Annual Boy Scout Elk Antler Auction during the month of May.

- Enjoy art and photo galleries, shopping, and local restaurants as you stroll through town.

- Mercill Archaeology Center located in the historic Coey Cabin at 105 Mercill Avenue.

- Snow King Mountain Resort located at 100 E. Snow King Avenue.
    - Alpine Slide
    - Horseback Riding
    - Hiking Trails
    - Paragliding

- On your way back up to the park, stop at the National Museum of Wildlife Art located 2.5 miles north of town on the west side of Highway 89.

Seven

WHERE TO STAY

There are several places to stay inside Grand Teton National Park along with some that are just outside the park. Other than the lodges located inside the park, this is not an all-inclusive list as there are other resorts outside of the park in Jackson Hole and many fabulous places to stay in the towns of Jackson and Wilson. Choosing a lodge can be difficult but I do not think you can go wrong with any resort inside the park. It all depends on what is important to you in your lodging.

If you are looking for a hotel style room then Jackson Lake Lodge is the place for you. It is the only lodge with rooms in the main lodge. If you want a swimming pool for the kids, then Jackson Lake Lodge is also the place to be as it has the only swimming pool in the park. The lodge offers many cabins which are really rustic style hotel rooms on the inside.

If you want to be right on the shore of a lake then you will want to stay at Signal Mountain Lodge, located on the shore of Jackson Lake and the only lodging directly on a lake inside the park. Looking for a western ranch experience? Then you will want to stay at the Triangle X Dude Ranch inside the park. If you think you have to have a television (why would you with so many things to do outdoors?) then you will need to stay outside of the park. Some resorts outside of the park also offer in room Internet service while you will have to go to the main lodge for Internet service if you stay inside the park.

All resorts will help you book outside activities like Snake River scenic float trips, guided fly fishing and lake fishing trips, horseback riding, scenic tours, and more. Some resorts offer activities of their own like the chuck wagon breakfast ride and Jackson Lake breakfast and dinner cruises booked through Jackson Lake Lodge. If you are planning a winter vacation to Grand Teton National Park, the Triangle X Dude Ranch is the only available lodging inside the park. The Hatchet Resort just outside of the park is also open. Both resorts operate on limited schedules during the winter season. Winter activities are concentrated near the town of Jackson and Teton Village.

For the campers out there, many park resorts also have campsites but not all. Under each resort heading, I have included whether camping is available for your convenience. Camping inside the park is on a first come, first serve basis. Be sure and check that the campgrounds you are looking at is equipped to handle your RV or camper. Warning! This is bear country so campers must take all bear safety precautions.

Where to Stay Inside the Park

View across Jackson Lake and the marina at Signal Mountain Lodge.

Signal Mountain Lodge
Season: Early May - Mid October
Campsites Also Available: Yes
Reservations: (307)543-2831 or Online
Website: signalmountainlodge.com

Signal Mountain Lodge is the only lodge in Grand Teton National Park located on Jackson Lake. The view of the Tetons across the lake is absolutely stunning. You cannot go wrong staying at any of the accommodations in the park but if you want to be right on Jackson Lake, Signal Mountain Lodge is the place for you. If you want to wake up every morning with coffee cup in hand and enjoy this gorgeous view, you will need to reserve a Lakefront Retreat as these are the only rooms with a view. That being said, any room at Signal Mountain Lodge is just a short walk to the beach.

Signal Mountain Lodge is the first lodge in the park to open and the last to close in the fall. The marina is open mid-May (or after ice out) through mid-September weather permitting to rent fishing boats, pontoons, canoes, and kayaks. The property features two restaurants. The casual Trapper Grill is open the entire season serving breakfast, lunch, and dinner. Be sure to try the Signal Mountain of Nachos but be forewarned, it is definitely a mountain. The intimate

Peaks Restaurant is open during the main season for when you are in the mood to dress up a little and enjoy the western bistro cuisine. The property also features two gift shops, a gas station, convenience store, and campgrounds. You can book many activities here like a scenic Snake River float trip (#1 recommended activity), guided fly fishing and lake fishing trips, and guided tours of Grand Teton and Yellowstone National Park.

On a personal note, I have stayed at the lodge several times now. My family absolutely loves it here, so much so that we request the same Lakefront Retreat every time we visit. I never tire of this view and honestly cannot imagine staying anywhere else but I am sure that is how everyone feels about where they stay as you just cannot go wrong staying anywhere in the park.

Savings Tip: If you are willing to chance the weather in the off season (May and October), you can save 30% on your lodging here by joining the Grand Teton Association for only $50. This also saves you 15% in gift shops operated by the association. You must have your membership card with you when you check in or shop to receive these benefits.

Interesting Fact: Signal Mountain Lodge was originally a hunting and fishing camp designed to attract wealthy outdoorsmen. Charles Wort purchased and expanded the lodging but sold the property to the Harris family in 1940 to pursue his dream of building a hotel in downtown Jackson. The Wort Hotel is still in operation today. The Harris family spent 40 years building Signal Mountain Lodge into what it is today.

View over the Willow Flats to Jackson Lake and the Grand Tetons from the Jackson Lake Lodge - a favorite spot for moose watching.

Jackson Lake Lodge

Season: Mid May - Early October
Campsites Also Available: No
Reservations: (800)628-9988
Website: www.gtlc.com/lodging/jackson-lake-lodge-overview.aspx

We have stayed at the Jackson Lake Lodge several times and the entire family loves it here. If you have children, they will enjoy having an outdoor pool (the only one in the park) to splash around in. The lodge sits on top of a bluff overlooking the Willow Flats with spectacular views across the water of Jackson Lake to the skyline of the Grand Tetons. The outdoor patio is a favorite spot to look for moose and other wildlife foraging in the Willow Flats. When I was a teenager, my younger sister and I would take the trail down to the pond and watch the beavers slap their tails at us while they were going about their business.

When you arrive at Jackson Lake Lodge, you are greeted at the doors by cowboys dressed in western finery and that sets the stage for your stay here. The upstairs lobby is a grand affair with a huge, oversize fireplace to relax in front of and towering, 60 foot picture windows framing the Teton Range, as well as a collection of Native American artifacts and Western art.

The lodge offers two dining experiences. The Mural room serves breakfast through dinner. I highly recommend you enjoy their breakfast buffet no matter where you are staying in the park. You will start your morning with a delicious assortment of fresh fruits and breakfast fare while enjoying the mountain scenery. If you are in the mood for fine dining, the menu has lot to offer and I have always enjoyed everything I have sampled here. If you do not feel like dressing up, the more casual Pioneer Grill is a counter style cafe open daily from 6:00 AM to 10:30 PM. Take a look around while you are in the Pioneer Grill. There are all sorts of old photos and artifacts on display from the area. For the adults, the Heron Cocktail Lounge features live entertainment, your favorite beverage and snacks, along with spectacular views.

The Jackson Lake Lodge offers 37 guests rooms as well as nearly 350 cottages. Guest facilities include news stand, gift and apparel shops, a large heated outdoor swimming pool, horseback riding, scenic Snake River float trips, breakfast and dinner cruises on Jackson Lake, chuck wagon rides to meals on the Willow Flats, guided lake and river fishing, tours of Grand Teton and Yellowstone National Parks, a gas station, and medical clinic.

Interesting Fact: Jackson Lake Lodge is located on the original site of the Amoretti Inn which was built in 1922. The Snake River Land Company purchased the lodge in 1930 and continued operations until 1953 when it was demolished to make way for Jackson Lake Lodge. The Snake River Land Company was formed by John D. Rockefeller Jr. to purchase land in Jackson Hole which he later donated to the federal government to form today's Grand Teton National Park. The original park only included the Grand Teton Range leaving out the valley and its lakes.

View across Jenny Lake to Cascade Canyon.

Jenny Lake Lodge

Season: June 1 - Early October
Campsites Also Available: Yes
Reservations: (800)628-9988
Website: www.gtlc.com/lodging/jenny-lake-lodge-overview.aspx

Jenny Lake is considered by many to be the most picturesque lake in Grand Teton National Park. Even if you do not stay here, you definitely need to visit and take in the beautiful views. This small, rustically elegant retreat sits quietly tucked amongst fragrant pines in the shadow of the Tetons. Situated at the base of the Tetons, Jenny Lake Lodge has provided a unique experience to travelers since the 1920s as well as the finest in service. The 37 Old West style historic cabins that make up Jenny Lake Lodge are beautifully appointed with down comforters and handmade quilts. There are no televisions or radios, and telephones are available upon request. The view of the mountains from the main lodge is spectacular with hiking trails and three lakes within easy walking distance.

The Jenny Lake Lodge is an all-inclusive resort and the only 4-diamond eco-resort in the park. Nightly rates include breakfast, five-course dinner, cycling, and horseback riding. Although the cabins at Jenny Lake are secluded, the lake itself receives a lot of traffic. Guests and visitors can rent canoes to paddle this pristine lake or catch a boat ride from the Jenny Lake boat dock to the base of Hidden Falls and Inspiration Point. This is a very popular activity in the park, accounting for a lot of the traffic. The facility boasts a huge parking lot for visitors, a visitor center, gift shop, bookstore, convenience store, and public restrooms.

Interesting Fact: The Jenny Lake Visitor Center is housed in the original studio of Harrison Crandall. Crandall was a famous photographer and artist who started his career taking photographs of wealthy dudes and dudines visiting in the park. John D. Rockefeller Jr.'s wife, Abigail, fell in love with the beauty of Jenny Lake. When her husband's land company purchased property around the area for park acquisition, she ordered many structures torn down because she thought they were marring the beauty of the landscape and interrupting the view.

View across the marina at Colter Bay, courtesy G. Edward Johnson.

Colter Bay Village
Season: Mid May - Early October
Campsites Also Available: Yes
Reservations: (800)628-9988
Website: www.gtlc.com/lodging/colter-bay-village-overview.aspx

Beautiful Colter Bay on Jackson Lake with Mount Moran and the Grand Tetons reflecting in the bay is one of the most picturesque places in the park. Colter Bay Village offers a unique lodging experience. The rustic cabins are original homestead cabins from the area that have been relocated here and renovated as guest accommodations. It has a large campground and RV resort offering shower and laundry facilities. The village offers a family restaurant, cafe court, gift shop, general store, gas station, convenience store, and marina. Book a breakfast or dinner cruise on Jackson Lake, rent a canoe, kayak or motor boat, or book a guided fishing trip. Even if you are not staying here, you will enjoy walking around the village, hiking the trails, browsing the gift shop, and spending some time in the newly renovated Colter Bay Visitor Center and Indian Arts Museum featuring interpretive displays of Native American artifacts from the David T. Vernon Collection, the most extensive collection in the National Park Service.

Tip: If you are planning a stay at Colter Bay, you may want to go earlier in the summer. Jackson Lake is a reservoir used to supply water down the Snake River into Idaho. Depending on the drought conditions there and the amount of water released from the lake, there are summers when Colter Bay is dry and the marina is closed. Reduced lake levels do not usually effect Colter Bay until sometime in August.

Interesting Fact: Colter Bay is named after explorer John Colter who was a member of the Lewis and Clark Expedition of 1804. In 1807, he worked for Manuel Lisa's trading post. Lisa sent Colter out to inform the Crow Indians of the trading post. His trek took him into Jackson Hole where he crossed the Teton Range in the winter of 1807-1808. He is believed to be the first Anglo-American to enter Jackson Hole and see the Grand Teton Mountains although his exact route is unknown. There is a monument dedicated to him on the shore of Colter Bay.

View from Triangle X Dude Ranch across the Snake River valley of Jackson Hole to the Grand Tetons.

Triangle X Dude Ranch
Summer: Mid May - October 31
Winter: Dec. 26 - Mid March
Campsites Also Available: No
Reservations: (307)733-2183
Website: trianglex.com

The first tourism in Jackson Hole began with the dude ranches. The Triangle X Ranch is the only dude ranch located within the National Park system and it is the oldest in Jackson Hole. The ranch was founded in 1926 when John and Maytie Turner purchased their homestead on Spread Creek. Descendants of the Turner family still operate the ranch today. If you are looking for an authentic dude ranch experience, the Triangle X is the place for you. The Triangle X is an all-inclusive resort located in the heart of Grand Teton National Park.

During the summer season, you will enjoy horseback riding, cookouts and square dancing along with scenic river float trips, hiking, fishing, and of course, beautiful scenery. In keeping with the dude ranch tradition, you can book a guided pack trip or big game hunt in the Teton Wilderness. Winter activities also abound at the Triangle X where you can go snowmobiling, snowshoeing, and cross country skiing then return to warm up in front of a cozy fireplace. During the peak summer season, the Triangle X requires a seven night stay, Sunday through Sunday.

Interesting Fact: Almost all of the dude ranches in Jackson Hole were originally started by settlers as cattle ranches. The climate and grazing conditions were not the best suited for this use and early settlers began taking in boarders. As the popularity of the automobile increased, so did the number of city tourists coming to Jackson Hole for the cowboy experience. Big game hunting was also a big draw and many early settlers supplemented their incomes by guiding hunters.

Spur Ranch Cabins at Dornan's
Season: Year Round
Campsites Also Available: No
Reservations: (307)733-2522
Website: dornans.com

The Spur Ranch Cabins are located at Dornan's on the banks of the Snake River. Their valley location offers unobstructed Teton views. Eight one-bedroom cabins and four two-bedroom duplexes are available along with the three-bedroom Spur Ranch House and Dornan Guest Cabin for long-term rental. The cabins all have fully equipped kitchens, queen beds, barbeques, and covered porches to enjoy the gorgeous views. With the Snake River in such close proximity, you can walk down and try your luck catching some trout to cook up on your grill.

Dornan's is a hub of activity during the summer months. Located in the heart of Menor's Ferry Historic District, you'll enjoy strolling through the Menor's Ferry property, the Chapel of the Transfiguration, Maud Noble's cabin, and visiting the Craig Thomas Discovery and Visitor Center. Amenities at Dornan's include a grocery store, deli, wine shop, and gift shop.

Dine outdoors at the Moose Chuckwagon while enjoying the local talent of the Hootenanny on Monday nights. Pizza, pasta, and sandwiches are also available at the Pizza Pasta Company restaurant. Fill up your gas tank before heading up to Yellowstone (45 miles away) or down to Jackson (only 12 miles away). Stop in at Adventure Sports to rent a canoe, kayak, or mountain bike. The multi-use pathway comes up from Jackson and leaves Dornan's for an eight mile trip to South Jenny Lake running alongside the Teton Park Road. During the winter months in Grand Teton National Park, Dornan's is just off of a maintained highway and is the perfect location for cross-country skiing and snowshoeing.

The plus side to staying here is having so much activity right at your fingertips. The down side for some people might be all the activity and traffic at this main intersection in the park during the peak season.

Savings Tip: If you are willing to chance the weather in the off season, you can save over 30% on your lodging here. Off season rates run from May 1-15th and October 16-31st.

Interesting Fact: Dornan's complex of lodging, restaurants, shops, and gas originally started out of the home of Evelyn Dornan. Evelyn took out her homestead in 1916. As tourist traffic to the Tetons and Yellowstone National Park started to increase, she and her son John began catering to passing travelers. Generation after generation of Dornan's have continued to build the tourist complex into what it is today.

Where to Stay Near the Park

View from the Hatchet Resort. This spectacular sunset interrupted our dinner at the Hatchet. It was simply the most stunning sunset I had ever seen and I had to try and capture it - breathtaking.

The Hatchet Resort
Season: Year Round
Campsites Also Available: No
Reservations: (877)543-2413
Website: hatchetresort.com

The Hatchet Resort is located just minutes from the east entrance to Grand Teton National Park in the Buffalo River Valley. Although I have not stayed here personally, I love the Hatchet. If I had to pin down what I love about it, it is the friendly, welcoming staff. More specifically it would be the people who run the restaurant. Now, most businesses are welcoming and friendly but this is that authentic feeling that you are welcome. That "Come on in and stay awhile," kind of feeling.

In 2013, my daughter and I visited the park in early spring. We walked into the restaurant shortly before 5:00 for dinner. They were not open yet, but guess what? Instead of turning us away, they invited us in to have a few cocktails with them before they opened. When my husband, son, and I were there on several occasions in late fall we enjoyed some very interesting conversations with Ron, who I believe is the chef and manager along with his girlfriend (she's great, too).

Did I mention that the food is delicious? It is! Within the immediate park area, the only restaurants you will find open during the early or late season are at the Hatchet and Signal Mountain Lodge. The Hatchet Resort features cabin lodging with Teton views from all cabins, two restaurants, gift shop, convenience store, gas station, and wireless Internet access. Many activities can be booked directly through the Hatchet Resort, including: Snake River raft rides, day or overnight horseback riding, guided Yellowstone tours, guided fly fishing, hiking, mountain biking, snowmobiling, snowshoeing, and hunting.

Interesting Fact: There were five original homesteaders making up the Hatchet Ranch and they were among some of the earliest homesteaders in Jackson Hole in 1892. The first settlers in Jackson Hole were John Carnes, his wife, and John Holland. They settled just south of the Gros Ventre River in 1884.

The Snake River near the Headwater's Lodge before an approaching storm.

Headwaters Lodge & Cabins at Flagg Ranch
Summer: June - September
Winter: Mid-December thru Early March
Campsites Also Available: Yes
Reservations: (800)443-2311
Website: www.gtlc.com/headwaters-lodge.aspx

The Headwaters Lodge & Cabins is uniquely situated between Grand Teton National Park and Yellowstone National Park on the John D. Rockefeller, Jr. Memorial Parkway. The cabins have all been recently renovated and feature outdoor patios with rocking chairs. They overlook the Snake River valley and provide quick access to hiking trails and fishing streams. We spent a lot of time fishing on the Snake River near the Headwaters Lodge and also tried our luck in nearby Polecat Creek up Grassy Lake Road, accessed from the lodge parking lot.

The property features a rustic lodge with a restaurant and bar, gift shop, gas station, and convenience store. The gas station and convenience store open the middle of May through mid-October and open again for the winter season, mid-December through mid-March. Activities include: Snake River raft rides, horseback riding, national park tours, guided fly fishing, and Yellowstone snowmobile tours in the winter. This is a beautiful location and facility. It is ideal if you are planning on visiting both parks. If there is any drawback, it would be that you do not have the view of the Tetons that you enjoy by staying in the park.

Interesting Fact: The Grassy Lake Road is also the old Ashton Freight Road used in the late 1800s to freight supplies by wagon from Idaho into Jackson Hole. Weather and road permitting, you can still take this road into Idaho but I would recommend a high clearance, four wheel drive vehicle.

The Gros Ventre landslide formed Lower Slide Lake in 1925. Aside from volcanic eruptions, the slide was one of the largest land mass movements in Earth's recent history.

Camping and RV Facilities

Campgrounds run by the National Park Service in Grand Teton National Park do not accept reservations and are on a first-come, first-serve basis. These include camping facilities at Jenny Lake, Signal Mountain, Colter Bay, Lizard Creek, and the Gros Ventre campground. Jenny Lake, Signal Mountain, and Colter Bay are usually the first to fill up. Lizard Creek campground is located in the northern end of Grand Teton National Park in a remote area near the northern end of Jackson Lake. The Gros Ventre campground is located along the Gros Ventre River on the southern edge of the park. It is a large facility that rarely fills up. The Colter Bay RV Park and Flagg Ranch (located just outside of the park) are concession run facilities and do take reservations.

Located on Highway 287/26 to the east and just outside of the park are the Hatchet Campground (run by the National Forest Service), Grand Teton Park Campground (www.yellowstonerv.com (307)543-2483), and Grand Teton Park RV Resort (307)733-1980.

Pacific Creek campground is located just outside of the park up Pacific Creek Road. On several trips to the park, grizzly bears and cubs have graced us with their presence near this road.

Another beautiful campground located in the Bridger-Teton National Forest is the Atherton Creek Campground on Lower Slide Lake. This campground is east of the southern end of Grand Teton National Park. Go north out of Kelly, Wyoming until you come to the Gros Ventre Road where you turn east. The road is paved to the campground. This is a very secluded area on a beautiful lake yet still close to the park activities. Further up the road are the smaller Red Hills and Crystal Creek campgrounds on the Gros Ventre River. Many of the above listed campgrounds are run by the National Forest Service. You can view a complete listing of their campgrounds in the area here: www.fs.usda.gov/activity/btnf/recreation/camping-cabins/.

Tip: Wherever you are planning on camping, please check ahead that the facility can handle your specific needs and be bear aware.

Interesting Fact: Lower Slide Lake was formed by the Gros Ventre landslide on July 23, 1925 when approximately 50,000,000 cubic yards of rock slid down Sheep Mountain. The rock field crossed the Gros Ventre River and continued up the opposing mountain side 300 feet, creating a natural dam on the Gros Ventre River which formed Lower Slide Lake.

Eight

WHERE TO EAT

Whether you are hungry for casual fare or fine cuisine, there is a restaurant in or near the park that will satiate your appetite. The following restaurants are all open during the main tourist season. If you are visiting the park early in the spring or later in the fall, your dining choices narrow down. The only restaurants open during this time are the ones at Signal Mountain Lodge and the Hatchett Resort. If you would like more variety during these times, head down to the town of Jackson for a myriad of choices.

In the early and late seasons, it will probably be dark during the drive back to your lodge. Be particularly vigilant watching for wildlife on the road after dark. Seriously, we have encountered elk and other wildlife on the road after dark almost every time we were returning home from dinner. For your safety and the animals, consider reducing your speed after dark to 10 miles below the posted speed limit. For your convenience, the restaurants are rated $-$$$ (least expensive - most expensive) and are in or near the park.

Jackson Lake Lodge

Mural Room - $$$
If you are looking for an upscale dining experience with breathtaking Teton views, the Mural Room is the place to go. The food is excellent and you cannot beat the Teton and Jackson Lake views through the floor to ceiling windows. Be sure to check out the murals on the back wall from which the restaurant derives its name. The murals were painted by Carl Roters, an American artist who won a competition in the 1950s to paint the murals which depict historical scenes from Jackson Hole.

Every morning in the Mural Room starts with a fabulous breakfast buffet which I highly recommend. The dinner menu features Rocky Mountain cuisine with items like elk tenderloin, buffalo, local trout, sustainable seafood, and scrumptious desserts. Lighter fare is featured on the lunch menu. Although a jacket and tie is not necessary, dressy casual would be appropriate attire. Reservations are recommended for dinner. Call (307) 543-3100 or reserve online at: www.gtlc.com/dining/jackson-lake-lodge-the-mural-room.aspx.

Breakfast Menu:
www.gtlc.com/GTLCSiteAssets/files/dining/Mural Room Breakfast 2014.pdf

Lunch Menu:
www.gtlc.com/GTLCSiteAssets/files/dining/Mural Room Lunch 2014.pdf

Dinner Menu:
www.gtlc.com/GTLCSiteAssets/files/dining/Mural Room Dinner 2014.pdf

Children's Menu:
www.gtlc.com/GTLCSiteAssets/files/dining/Kids Menu 2014.pdf

Dessert Menu:
www.gtlc.com/GTLCSiteAssets/files/dining/Mural Room Dessert 2014.pdf

Pioneer Grill - $

If you are getting ready to hit the hiking trail or have just returned from a fishing expedition, the casual Pioneer Grill is for you. Serving breakfast, lunch, and dinner, the Pioneer Grill boasts the longest continual soda fountain counter still in use today. You could spend a lot of time in this restaurant checking out all of the pioneer artifacts and historical photos of early life in Jackson Hole. Enjoy a buffalo burger, bowl of chili, meatloaf, trout, hot sandwiches and more. The Pioneer Grill is known for its delicious milkshakes made from homemade ice cream. Reservations are not necessary and take-out is available.

Breakfast Menu:
www.gtlc.com/GTLCSiteAssets/files/dining/Pioneer Grill Breakfast Menu 2014.pdf

Lunch & Dinner Menu:
www.gtlc.com/GTLCSiteAssets/files/dining/Pioneer Lunch-Dinner Menu 2014.pdf

Children's Menu:
www.gtlc.com/GTLCSiteAssets/files/dining/Kids Menu 2014.pdf

Blue Heron Lounge - $$

The Blue Heron Lounge was voted the "Best Watering Hole - Human Division" by the National Park Foundation and features an outdoor balcony to sit back and relax while you enjoy your beverage. Food service includes a limited menu of sandwiches, finger foods, soup, and salad. Open daily from 11:00-11:00.

Food Menu:
www.gtlc.com/GTLCSiteAssets/files/dining/Blue Heron 2014.pdf

Drink Menu:
www.gtlc.com/GTLCSiteAssets/files/dining/Blue Heron Bar Drink Menu 2014.pdf

Poolside Cafe - $ and Pool BBQ - $$
Jackson Lake Lodge boasts the park's only in-ground swimming pool. There is no need to cut the kiddo's swimming time short when you can dine poolside. The poolside cafe features grilled sandwiches, pizza, salads, and ice cream. In the evening, it turns into an outdoor barbeque featuring smoked brisket, chicken, ribs, hamburgers, veggie burgers, and salad bar. Live music is performed nightly.

Poolside Cafe Menu:
www.gtlc.com/GTLCSiteAssets/files/dining/Poolside Menu 11.pdf

Pool BBQ Menu:
www.gtlc.com/GTLCSiteAssets/files/dining/Pool BBQ 11 New.pdf

The above menus are 2014 menus and are subject to change.

Jenny Lake Lodge - $$$

The Jenny Lake Lodge dining room provides an intimate setting for a special dinner. It is an example of rustic elegance at its finest. The Jenny Lake Lodge is an all-inclusive resort. As such, it offers five different nightly menus featuring five-course dinners. Included on the menus are items like grilled watermelon steak, pan seared scallops and prawns, hoisin glazed pork belly, buffalo carpaccio, seafood ceviche, braised rabbit gnocchi, pancetta wrapped sturgeon, duck leg confit, paella, espresso rubbed elk loin, and more. Breakfast and lunch are served daily. This is the most expensive place to eat in the park. Jackets are recommended for dinner and reservations are required for breakfast, lunch, and dinner. For reservations call: (307) 733-4647

Breakfast Menu
www.gtlc.com/GTLCSiteAssets/files/dining/2014 JNY breakfast menu-2.pdf

Lunch Menu
www.gtlc.com/GTLCSiteAssets/files/dining/2014 JNY Lunch Menu.pdf

Wine Menu
www.gtlc.com/GTLCSiteAssets/files/dining/JNY Wine List 2012.pdf

Nightly Dinner Menu 1
www.gtlc.com/GTLCSiteAssets/files/dining/2014 JNY Dinner Menu 1.pdf

Nightly Dinner Menu 2
www.gtlc.com/GTLCSiteAssets/files/dining/2014 JNY Dinner Menu 2.pdf

Nightly Dinner Menu 3
www.gtlc.com/GTLCSiteAssets/files/dining/2014 JNY Dinner Menu 3.pdf

Nightly Dinner Menu 4
www.gtlc.com/GTLCSiteAssets/files/dining/2014 JNY Dinner
Menu 4.pdf

Nightly Dinner Menu 5
www.gtlc.com/GTLCSiteAssets/files/dining/2014 JNY Dinner
Menu 5.pdf

   The above menus are 2014 menus and are subject to change.

Colter Bay Village

Ranch House Restaurant - $$
The Ranch House Restaurant at Colter Bay Village was remodeled in 2009 to reflect the western, homesteader history of the park. Historic photos adorn the walls and the new bar has area ranch brands burned into the top. This is a casual restaurant that the entire family will enjoy. The cuisine has a western flare featuring items like honey habanero wings, Paintbrush Canyon salad, smoked portabellas, barbecue beef brisket, and more. The Ranch House is open daily for breakfast from 6:30-10:30, lunch from 11:30-1:30, and dinner from 5:30-9:00. Attire is casual and no reservations are required.

Breakfast Menu:
gtlc.com/GTLCSiteAssets/files/dining/RH_Breakfast_2014.pdf

Lunch Menu:
www.gtlc.com/GTLCSiteAssets/files/dining/RH_Lunch_2014.pdf

Dinner Menu:
www.gtlc.com/GTLCSiteAssets/files/dining/RH_Dinner_2014.pdf

Children's Menu:
www.gtlc.com/GTLCSiteAssets/files/dining/RH_Childrens_Menu_2014.pdf

John Colter Cafe Court - $
If you are looking for a quick meal or want to take a picnic lunch on the trail, stop in to the John Colter Cafe Court at Colter Bay Village. The cafe features American and Mexican cuisine, sandwiches, salads, hamburgers, and ice cream. Open daily from 10:00 a.m. to 10:00 p.m.

The above menus are 2014 menus and are subject to change.

Signal Mountain Lodge

The Peaks Restaurant - $$$

The Peaks Restaurant is a small, intimate restaurant overlooking Jackson Lake and the Tetons. Signal Mountain Lodge is the only lodge in the park that is on the shore of Jackson Lake. The restaurant is separated from the Deadman's Bar lounge by a large stone fireplace that sure feels good on a chilly evening. The restaurant is only open for dinner and serves up western bistro fare with items like baked trout, pan-seared elk, bison burgundy, organic vegetable risotto, and more.

During peak season, check at the front desk to see if dinner reservations are required. The Peaks Restaurant does close a week or so earlier in the season than the Trapper Grill (below) but Signal Mountain Lodge is the only lodge in the park open until mid-October. If you want to be right on Jackson Lake for a romantic, fireside dinner, The Peaks is for you. A jacket is not required but I would recommend dressy casual attire.

Dinner Menu:

signalmountainlodge.com/filemanager_v4/foreverresorts_v4/1/119/it ems/40F18F27-CE36-A609-55ED1C306FB25337.pdf

Trapper Grill - $$

The Trapper Grill opens daily at 7:00 for breakfast, lunch, and dinner. This is a more casual, family friendly environment than The Peaks. It is perfect for starting your day before you hit the hiking trail, stopping in for a quick sandwich at lunch, and ending a day of fishing — no need to get dressed up if you do not feel like it. Starting your day looking to the Tetons over Jackson Lake cannot be beat and the breakfasts are delicious. On a side note, I would recommend trying the blackberry stuffed French toast. It is divine.

In addition to burgers, the lunch/dinner menu is full of wonderful sandwiches like cran-pesto turkey and Hidden Falls hummus. Dinner entrees include, tequila lime chicken quesadilla, Oxbow Bend burrito, baby back ribs, and more. One menu item you must try while you are here is the Signal Mountain of Nachos. They advertise this as a meal for a crowd and believe me, it is definitely a mountain of nachos! If two people are splitting these nachos, you really truly will only need the half order. This is the only restaurant open in the park until the lodge closes in mid-October.

Breakfast Menu:
signalmountainlodge.com/filemanager_v4/foreverresorts_v4/1/119/it ems/40E0653D-C934-EDD7-63B219CC33CB3B38.pdf

Lunch & Dinner Menu:
signalmountainlodge.com/filemanager_v4/foreverresorts_v4/1/119/it ems/40F25E5B-DE19-4FA3-CF8ABF91410F1462.pdf

Children's Menu:
signalmountainlodge.com/filemanager_v4/foreverresorts_v4/1/119/it ems/40E84197-F3DC-05AB-3BD6B0A6B3D967A9.pdf

Gluten Free Menu:
signalmountainlodge.com/filemanager_v4/foreverresorts_v4/1/119/it ems/450A2E7D-061D-C9C8-066AD0C41DD923D7.pdf

Deadman's Bar - $$
Deadman's Bar is the lounge at Signal Mountain Lodge. Domestic, local, regional, and organic microbrews are on tap along with any other libation you might prefer. Food service is also available in the lounge from the Trapper Grill lunch & dinner menu above.

Wine List:
signalmountainlodge.com/filemanager_v4/foreverresorts_v4/1/119/it ems/40F5F5DF-00D7-1DF2-789DBA4BAE555416.pdf

The above menus are 2014 menus and are subject to change.

Hatchet Resort

Hatchet Grill and Whetstone Lodge - $$
The Hatchet Grill and Whetstone Lodge share the same menu. The Grill is open for breakfast, lunch, and dinner while the Whetstone is only open for dinner. The Whetstone is often booked for private parties but when it is not, it is one of my favorite places to eat in Jackson Hole. Start your day with a satisfying breakfast or stop in for a bowl of chili (I highly recommend the chili) and a sandwich for lunch. If there is not a private party, dine at the Whetstone for dinner. The rustic log restaurant features a fireplace, wildlife mounts, and historical photos of the Hatchet.

The Hatchet Resort is named after the Hatchet Cattle Ranch first homesteaded in 1892 by John and Lucy Shive. The Shive's were amongst the earliest settlers in Jackson Hole. They joined forces with four other homesteaders to form the Hatchet Cattle Ranch and the ranch has been an operating ranch ever since. This down-home feel comes across in the hospitality of the Whetstone's managers. Be sure to ask them to make you a huckleberry marguerita, they are to die for. You may not want to stop at one so be sure to have a designated driver.

A few dishes that I highly recommend are the seared rainbow trout, elk medallions with portabella demi glaze, rib-eye steak, and fettuccini alfredo. Did I mention the chili? Honestly, you cannot go wrong here. My family has had everything on their menu by now and it is all delicious. Reservations are not necessary although you might want to call ahead to make sure the Whetstone is not closed for a private party, 877-543-2413. The dress code is casual.

Breakfast Menu: hatchetresort.com/grill.breakfast.php
Lunch Menu: hatchetresort.com/grill.lunch.php
Dinner Menu: hatchetresort.com/grill.dinner.php

The above menus are 2014 menus and are subject to change.

Headwaters Lodge at Flagg Ranch

Sheffields Restaurant and Saloon - $$

Located just north of Grand Teton National Park on John D. Rockefeller Jr. Memorial Parkway at the Headwaters Lodge, Sheffields Restaurant is the perfect place to stop for breakfast on your way to Yellowstone National Park or when returning home for dinner. The restaurant features western cuisine and more with items like bison & elk meatloaf, rustic bison potpie, caramelized goat cheese, and Teddy Roosevelt's bison and elk chili. Seared local trout is on the menu and you can even have your catch of cleaned trout cooked by the chef if brought to the restaurant by 3:00 p.m. The restaurant is open daily and has a casual, western atmosphere. As such, the attire is casual and reservations are not necessary. The restaurant is also open during the winter snowmobiling season from mid-December to early March. Phone: (800) 443-2311

Breakfast Menu:
www.gtlc.com/GTLCSiteAssets/files/main/Flagg Breakfast 2014.pdf

Lunch Menu:
www.gtlc.com/GTLCSiteAssets/files/main/Flagg Lunch 2014.pdf

Dinner Menu:
www.gtlc.com/GTLCSiteAssets/files/main/Flagg Dinner 2014.pdf

Bar Menu:
gtlc.com/GTLCSiteAssets/files/main/Flagg Saloon Food 2014.pdf

The above menus are 2014 menus and are subject to change.

Leek's Marina & Pizzeria

Leek's Pizzeria - $

Sometimes when you are on vacation and you have dined many nights out at fancy restaurants, a good old-fashioned pizza really sounds good. Leek's Pizzeria fits the bill deliciously! The marina and pizzeria is located towards the northern end of Jackson Lake. To get there drive approximately 2 miles north of the Colter Bay turnout on the John D. Rockefeller Jr. Memorial Parkway. There are many specialty pizzas and calzones on the menu or you can create your own. Try the pesto sticks for starters. There are also several sandwiches to choose from, spaghetti and meatballs, and a children's menu. In addition to soft drinks, beer and wine are served. Leek's Pizzeria opens later in May and closes for the season early in September.

Menu:
signalmountainlodge.com/filemanager_v4/foreverresorts_v4/1/119/items/40EBE3BE-0AF9-C335-D916C9D95D1648AC.pdf

The above menus are 2014 menus and are subject to change.

Dornan's at Moose

Moose Chuckwagon - $$

Start your day off with a hearty breakfast around the campfire in the tepee or dine outdoors at the Chuckwagon. When you are through with breakfast, stop into the grocery, deli, and wine shops to pack a picnic lunch for the day. Dinner at the Chuckwagon is a western affair cooked in Dutch ovens and served over an open campfire, featuring beef stew, BBQ beef short ribs, panko crusted rainbow trout, prime rib on Sunday's, salad bar, and dessert.

Monday nights feature the Local Hootenanny. Be there between 5:00-6:00 p.m. if you would like to perform, otherwise enjoy the show. The Chuckwagon opens the second Saturday in June and stays open through Labor Day for breakfast, lunch, and dinner, however it is closed for private events on Friday and Saturday nights. It is open farther into September for breakfast and lunch as long as the weather permits. Phone: (307) 733-2415 ext. 305

Chuckwagon Breakfast, Lunch, and Dinner Menu:

dornans.com/dining/chuckwagon/menu/

The Pizza Pasta Company - $$

If you are in the mood for Italian cuisine, the Pizza Pasta Company will not disappoint. Start your dinner off with moose bread, baked brie with raspberry jalapeno compote, blue bacon stuffed mushrooms and more. Build your own calzones and pizzas or try one of their specialties, like the Mount Moran (garlic cream, chicken, roma tomatoes, spinach, and pine nuts) or the Mount Owen (sun-dried pesto, mozzarella, asiago, feta, and Gouda). There are also many delicious pasta dishes, buffalo Bolognese, Florentine ravioli, red curry chicken, and more, along with sandwiches. The restaurant hours vary daily. Phone: (307) 733-2415 ext. 204

The Pizza Pasta Company Menu:
dornans.com/dining/pizzapasta/menu/

Monday Hours: 11:30 a.m. - 3:00 p.m.
5:00-7:00 p.m. for the Local Hootenanny
Tuesday, Wednesday, Thursday Hours: 11:30 a.m. - 3:00 p.m.
Friday, Saturday, Sunday Hours: 11:30 a.m. - 7:00 p.m.

The above menus are 2014 menus and are subject to change.

Nine

QUICK REFERENCE

Below are some suggested items you might consider packing for hiking and other miscellaneous activities, followed by alphabetical business listings with phone numbers and website addresses for lodging, restaurants, and activities.

Consider Packing the Following Items

Hiking
- Trail Map
- Compass
- Bear Spray (Keep it readily accessible. Do not stuff it inside your backpack.)
- Backpack
- Bottled Water
- Snacks
- Jackets (Dress in layers when hiking into the mountains.)
- Appropriate Shoes
- Camera

Miscellaneous Items
- Collapsible Chairs (These are nice if you are going to spend some time wildlife watching.)
- Camera Tripod
- Small Cooler (For packing lunches or snacks.)
- Fishing Poles and Tackle Box
- Golf Clubs
- Tennis Rackets

Lodging & Camping Listing

Colter Bay Village
800-628-9990
www.gtlc.com/lodging/colter-bay-village-overview.aspx

Colter Bay Village RV Park
800-628-9988
www.gtlc.com/lodging/colter-bay-village-rv-park.aspx

Grand Teton Park Campgrounds
307-543-2483
www.yellowstonerv.com/

Grand Teton Park RV Resort
307-733-1980

Hatchet Resort
877-543-2413
hatchetresort.com/

Headwaters Lodge & Cabins at Flagg Ranch
800-443-2311
www.gtlc.com/headwaters-lodge.aspx

Jackson Lake Lodge
800-628-9988
www.gtlc.com/lodging/jackson-lake-lodge-overview.aspx

Jenny Lake Lodge
800-628-9989
www.gtlc.com/lodging/jenny-lake-lodge-overview.aspx

Signal Mountain Lodge
307-543-2831
signalmountainlodge.com/

Spur Ranch Cabins at Dornan's
307-733-2522
dornans.com/

Teton Covered Wagon Train
888-734-6101
www.tetonwagontrain.com/

Triangle X Dude Ranch
307-733-2183
trianglex.com/

Restaurant Listing

Dornan's Moose Chuckwagon
307-733-2415 ext. 305
dornans.com/dining/chuckwagon/menu/

Dornan's Pizza Pasta Company
307-733-2415 ext. 304
dornans.com/dining/pizzapasta/menu/

Hatchet Resort – Grill & Whetstone
877-543-2413
hatchetresort.com/grill.php

Jackson Lake Lodge – Blue Heron Lounge
307-201-1332
www.gtlc.com/dining/jackson-lake-lodge-blue-heron-lounge.aspx

Jackson Lake Lodge – Mural Room
307-543-3100
www.gtlc.com/dining/jackson-lake-lodge-the-mural-room.aspx

Jackson Lake Lodge – Pioneer Grill
307-543-2811
www.gtlc.com/dining/jackson-lake-lodge-pioneer-grill.aspx

Jackson Lake Lodge – Pool Side Café & BBQ
307-543-2811
www.gtlc.com/dining/jackson-lake-lodge-coffee.aspx

Jenny Lake Lodge
307-733-4647
www.gtlc.com/lodging/jenny-lake-lodge-dining.aspx

Leek's Marina & Pizzeria
307-543-2831
signalmountainlodge.com/signal-mountain-dining

Signal Mountain Lodge – Deadman's Bar
307-543-2831
signalmountainlodge.com/signal-mountain-dining

Signal Mountain Lodge – Peaks
307-543-2831
signalmountainlodge.com/signal-mountain-dining

Signal Mountain Lodge – Trapper Grill
307-543-2831
signalmountainlodge.com/signal-mountain-dining

Activities Listing

AlpenGlow Tours
307-739-1914
www.alpenglowtours.com/

Colter Bay Visitor Center & Indian Arts Museum
307-739-3594
www.nps.gov/grte/planyourvisit/hours.htm

Eco Tour Adventures
307-690-9533
www.jhecotouradventures.com/

Exum Guide Service & School of Mountaineering
307-733-2297
exumguides.com/

Grizzly Country Wildlife Adventures
307-413-4389
grizzlycountrywildlifeadventures.com/

Jackson Hole & Greater Yellowstone Visitor Center
307-733-3316
www.fws.gov/nwrs/threecolumn.aspx?id=2147509813

Jackson Hole Historical Society & Museum
307-733-2414
www.jacksonholehistory.org/

Jackson Hole Wildlife Safaris
307-690-6402
jacksonholewildlifesafaris.com/

Laurance S. Rockefeller Preserve
307-739-3654
www.nps.gov/grte/planyourvisit/lsr.htm

Lewis & Clark River Expeditions
800-824-5375
www.lewisandclarkriverrafting.com/

Miller Ranch
307-733-3316
www.fws.gov/nwrs/threecolumn.aspx?id=2147509832

Murie Center
307-739-2246
muriecenter.org/

National Elk Refuge
307-733-3316
www.fws.gov/refuge/national_elk_refuge/

Scenic Safaris
888-734-8898
www.scenic-safaris.com/

The Hole Picture
208-709-3250 or 208-483-2420
www.the-hole-picture.com/

Tram at Jackson Hole Mountain Resort
307-739-2654
www.jacksonhole.com/

VIP Adventure Travel
307-699-1077
www.vipadventuretravel.com/

Wildlife Expeditions of Teton Science Schools
877-404-6626
www.tetonscience.org/wildlife-expeditions

Other Books by Kendra Leah Fuller

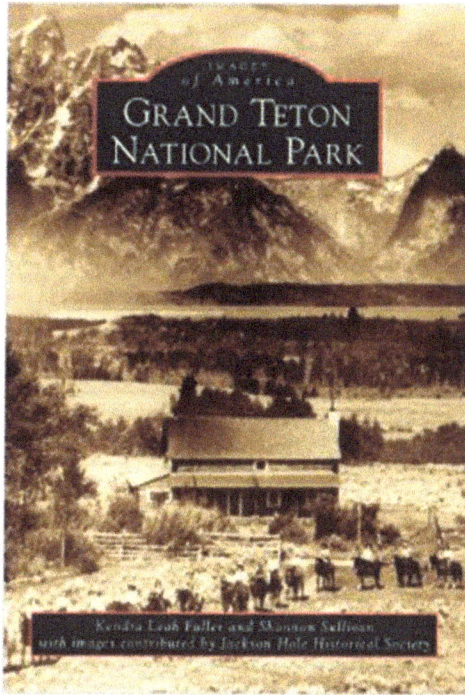

The majestic beauty of Grand Teton National Park has moved people throughout time. Native Americans believed in the spiritual power of the towering mountain peaks and journeyed there to gain special powers. Early fur traders, who had just crossed less ominous mountain ranges, viewed with trepidation the massive obstacle that loomed before them on their passage to the Pacific Northwest. In others, the Tetons ignited vision and passion - a vision to preserve for all generations to come and a passion to protect the independent way of life known by the first settlers of this western frontier.

      The formation of Grand Teton National Park spanned the course of nearly 70 years. Although there were many people who shared the struggle before them, it was not until Stephen Mather and Horace M. Albright took up the fight in 1915 that steps towards success were taken. Albright's tenacity and ability to convey his vision to philanthropist John D. Rockefeller Jr. set in motion a very long journey that culminated with Pres. Harry S. Truman signing today's Grand Teton National Park into existence on September 13, 1950.

Preview on Amazon: www.amazon.com/dp/1467131482/

About the Author

Kendra Leah Fuller is an author and freelance writer. Born and raised a city girl, she now lives in small town America with her family. She enjoys traveling and photography, relaxing by a lake with fishing pole in hand, and sitting around a campfire with family and friends.

Ms. Fuller has a lifelong love of writing. She is currently working on her first novel. A serial entrepreneur, she also writes on a variety of different business topics designed to help small business owners find success online, through her blog at www.writerkendraleah.com. She also writes under the pen name Kendra Leah.

Connect With the Author:
Website: www.writerkendraleah.com
Facebook: www.facebook.com/WriterKendraLeah
Twitter: @Writing2Day
Pinterest: www.pinterest.com/authorklfuller
Google+: plus.google.com/100101810474378518308

Plan Your Trip To
Grand Teton National Park

- [ ] Snake River Raft Ride
- [ ] Jackson Lake Boat Cruise
- [ ] Chuck Wagon Breakfast Ride
- [ ] Relax for a while at Oxbow Bend
- [ ] Drive to the top of Signal Mountain
- [ ] Hike to Hidden Falls, Inspiration Point, Cascade Canyon
- [ ] Hike to a Mountain Lake
- [ ] Fly Fishing/Jackson Lake Guided Fishing Trip
- [ ] Moose-Wilson Road to take the Tram from Teton Village
- [ ] Take a Day Trip to Yellowstone National Park

www.WriterKendraLeah.com

Easy Hikes - Big Rewards
Grand Teton National Park

- ☐ Colter Bay Lakeshore Trail, 2.0 Miles
- ☐ Heron Pond & Swan Lake, 3.0 Miles
- ☐ Willow Flats, 4.9 or 8.3 Mile Loop
- ☐ String Lake, 3.4 Mile Loop
- ☐ Taggart Lake, 4.0 Mile Loop
- ☐ Leigh Lake, 5.6 Miles
- ☐ Jenny Lake, 7.7 Mile Loop
- ☐ Hidden Falls from Boat Dock, 0.2 Miles
- ☐ Inspiration Point from Boat Dock, 0.4 Miles
- ☐ Cascade Canyon from Boat Dock, 9.8 Roundtrip

WWW.WRITERKENDRALEAH.COM

www.ingramcontent.com/pod-product-compliance
Lightning Source LLC
Chambersburg PA
CBHW041259040426
42334CB00028BA/3081